T0051107

THE POWER OF WHY

THE POWER OF WHY

Breaking Out in a Competitive Marketplace

C. RICHARD WEYLMAN

With a Foreword by Greg Ostergren

amazonpublishing

Published by Amazon Publishing
P.O. Box 400818
Las Vegas, NV 89140

ISBN-13: 9781477800737
ISBN-10: 1477800735

Dedicated to all the men and women who go to the marketplace every day committed to their success and that of their enterprise.

Contents

Acknowledgments

I need to thank so many people who have helped guide and produce this book. Were it not for them, I could never have written it.

God, for the title and his many blessings that led me to share this with you.

My wife, Sylvie, who encouraged and supported me throughout this long process and thought I should add another chapter: "Why I Love My Wife." But that would require another book!

Laurie Anderson and her daughter, Janelle, who retyped these words so many times that several perfectly good sets of nails were sacrificed.

My executive team, Teri, Jim, Dick, Michael, and Deb, who "ran the show" while I wrote these words for you.

Alan Rinzler, for his help as a developmental editor — without his guidance you wouldn't have what is in your hand.

The many clients who, by believing in our work, helped us find the pathway to elevate your business performance in today's marketplace.

Also to our "kids," who kept me laughing even when I was stuck: Chanel, Tiffany, Rolex, Jimmy Choo, and Boulie. They are our menagerie and family.

Foreword

R ICHARD WEYLMAN COMPLETELY CHANGED how the American National Insurance Company Multiple Line Division thinks about our approach to markets, and the delivery of our products and services to our clients. What he taught us has proven to be invaluable in helping us distinguish ourselves with our best clients and prospects and drive our success in a very competitive marketplace.

Richard and his firm helped us realize that we were thinking as merchandisers with our products as markets rather than as true marketers serving people. The insight and lessons that we gained from Richard are now at the very foundation of our long-term strategy and annual business plans.

American National Insurance Company was founded in 1905 and is headquartered in Galveston, Texas. Our company has multiple subsidiaries, with operations in Springfield, Missouri; Glenmont, New York; League City, Texas; and San Antonio, Texas. Strong management and prudent reinvestment in the company's growth have made American National a major provider of insurance and annuities. We offer a broad variety of life insurance, retirement annuities, accident and health insurance, pension plan products and services, credit insurance, and property and casualty (P&C) insurance for personal lines, agribusiness, and targeted commercial exposures.

Our products are sold in all fifty states and Puerto Rico, although not all products are offered in every jurisdiction. Products are distributed through career agents, independent marketing organizations, and multiple line exclusive agents as well as direct distribution channels. American National's mission is to be the company of choice for insurance and other financial products and services, while maintaining superior financial strength. Assets total over $22 billion with property/casualty premiums of over $1 billion annually. And we're proud to say that American National has paid dividends to shareholders every year since 1911.

I'm in charge of all the property/casualty home office operations and all the multiple line exclusive and career life agents for American National. We currently have over twelve hundred multiple line exclusive agents writing property/casualty, life, and annuities and over three hundred career life agents. Prior to meeting Richard, we were already one of the top companies in cross-selling our property/casualty and life insurance products to our clients and serving their insurance needs. Richard helped take us to the next level.

I first met Richard when we asked him to speak at our annual Professional Seminar, where we bring in our agents from across the country for several days of educational and training sessions. He was a big hit with our agents and home office executive staff. We had him speak again at the next Professional Seminar. Richard laid out for us how agents and companies often jump from one market to the next, never becoming well known or developing deep relationships in any market. In such an approach, every new client becomes a painful and expensive experience to obtain.

We knew we had to change our approach. We began to realize that a significant threat to the insurance industry was the industry itself, which was becoming a real race to the bottom. Many insurance companies seemed hell-bent on commoditizing insurance products by heavily advertising saving money over every other company without real consideration and understanding for a family's or small business's personal needs. Unfortunately, as a result of companies and agents being of no real value to them, more consumers began moving in the direction of buying no insurance. After all, the cheapest insurance is no insurance!

Consequently, we concluded that for us to achieve the next level of success, we needed to fully embrace and incorporate the Power of Why concept espoused by Richard Weylman. We didn't have hundreds of millions to spend on advertising but we knew of many companies making such expenditures that were having just as difficult a time achieving growth. We also didn't want to be a part of the race to the bottom.

Therefore, we contracted with Richard's team to integrate his methods into our multiple line and career life agent distribution systems. The process was multifaceted and took about thirty months. Working with our top clients and Richard's team, we articulated our Unique Value Promise (UVP). This was something we were already doing and was the reason our top clients stated that they continue to do business with us over all the others. The real breakthrough, though, was being able to articulate our UVP to prospects and newer clients so that we multiplied our best clients. There's no better path to success than multiplying your best clients!

There were a number of times during the process when Richard looked at me and said, "You're thinking like a merchandiser!" As a leader in a company that prides itself on making a meaningful and positive difference in peoples' lives, that was difficult to hear. I now think as a marketer serving our clients, not as a merchandiser.

Richard helped open our eyes to the almost limitless number of true markets and market potential. His wisdom and the Power of Why process are now a fundamental part of our new-agents training and our strategic and operational planning.

I'm an avid reader of business books, and am certain that you'll find Richard Weylman's concepts extremely practical, unique, and effective. I'm proud to recommend Richard's book to anyone who seeks to gain a lasting competitive edge in prospecting for new clients while building deeper, more rewarding relationships with your best customers.

GREGORY V. OSTERGREN

Executive Vice President, Director of Multiple Line,

ANICO Chairman, President & CEO,

American National Property and Casualty Company

Chairman, Farm Family Companies

Part I

DEFINING YOUR UNIQUE VALUE PROMISE

1

Why Asking "Why?" Will Work for You

ASKING "WHY" IS THE FIRST step in my approach to consulting with a business executive, coaching a sales or marketing team, finding out what's working and what isn't in any organization, and helping any company achieve its goals.

Asking why is also a good way to begin this book, starting with our title. Let's begin with that promise. Why is this book going to help you solve your business problems and break out in a competitive marketplace?

First, let's be clear that by breaking out we don't mean just getting ahead and leading the pack. No, indeed. What we want to achieve is leaving the entire pack of competitors in the dust, far behind.

That's our goal here: to elevate your business performance and presence so that you are the best and only choice for your product and services — regardless of your geographic footprint or your vertical or target markets. This book is intended to help you and your organization reach the point of truly "breaking out in a competitive marketplace."

If you ask why, then ask again, and then again, you can discover the truth about solving any problem in business. This works for every aspect of your company, from building a team to product development to sales and customer retention.

You already have plenty of questions, I'm sure. You've bought this book with a goal in mind and have a list of your own. But let's begin with a few suggestions so you that can get an idea of how to organize the Power of Why and move forward with each new question building on the answers you're receiving.

Good Questions

How can I break out in a competitive marketplace?

Here are three questions we can begin with and some typical answers I've heard:

1. *Why are your customers buying from you right now?*

"I was first to market. For eighteen months now there's been no other product available that's exactly like mine. But my competitor is gearing up to come out with something we hear is very close, and maybe better, so my product development team is scratching to get a prototype and see how we can top it."

"I have the lowest price. But my gross margins are way down and I'm not making enough net profit."

"Our distribution is tops. We're in every tech store in the country. But an upstart from out of nowhere is selling online, so every day he's chipping away at my base."

2. *Are your customers staying with you or shopping around, and if the latter, why?*

"We're pretty good at bringing them in, but the customer 'fickle level' is intense and we can't figure it out. Sometimes it looks like a revolving door to me. They're coming in, then turning around and going out, and we usually don't see them again."

"Our research shows a customer retention rate of only 64 percent. I'm guessing it's because of negligible differences in price, platform, product specs, packaging, and customer service. But I don't really know why they leave."

"The stick-with-us level is pretty flat, and we've got to increase it to get out ahead of our competition."

3. *What is it about your competition's relationship to their customers that you haven't figured out yet? Why are they so successful?*

"I really don't know why. Our sales team is as good as theirs, but they're definitely gaining more customers and keeping them in the family longer. In fact, forever! How do they do that?"

"I wish I knew. We need to do a better sales job, so I tried to hire their COO away from my biggest competitor, but he just smiled and said no thanks."

"We're not nearly as big or well known yet as most of our competitors, but I know we can catch up and pass the whole pack. I'm trying to find a new approach that we can afford that will give us a kick start."

The Value of Our Preliminary Answers

All of the answers so far identify overriding problems that lead to one precise goal: to increase your number of customers and keep them in the fold. No one wants a customer who's just passing through, constantly shopping for the small incremental incentives that you or one of your competitors may be offering. This kind of consumer is what I call "loyalty neutral." They don't particularly care whom they buy from and have no devotion to any one brand, retail outlet, supplier, or client service.

What we'd all prefer, I'm sure you'll agree, is a customer who would never think of changing, who is completely committed to you and what you provide for them. The challenge is how to reach, capture, and keep this type of customer whom I define as "delighted advocates."

To accomplish this, your job is to transform your company into a customer-centric organization. I've found that customers hunger for businesses that are genuinely focused on making a difference in their lives, and not just on making a buck. Unfortunately, most of us in business are so focused on making a buck that we miss what's happening on a daily basis with our customers. Well-intentioned executives in front office, marketing, and sales find themselves struggling to achieve a deep understanding of the real reasons why customers inquire, buy, and remain loyal to a business today. Their marketing and sales messaging and their service deliverables are primarily focused on business performance or product offerings. They're company-centric rather than customer-centric. So they're not yet creating real loyalty and delighted advocacy.

That is the premise of this book. The relentless focus by businesses to achieve growth by touting who they are or how they are good has had disastrous effects on growth, customer retention, and marketplace distinction. Consequently, discounting has replaced value — which has gone to zero!

Adopting and consistently delivering a customer-centric perspective in marketing, sales, and service profoundly elevates business performance throughout every aspect of your organization. That's what this book is about.

There are many facets to this process, which I'll explain in detail in this book. Individually, they are significant. Together, they will enable any business or professional to break out in the competitive, commoditized environment we know as the world of business today.

This leads to our next question:

> *What happens when you turn loyalty neutral customers into delighted advocates?*

We've all experienced advocacy, or, if you will, passionate devotion, and I don't mean just with our family, friends, and co-workers. I've been in love with Peet's Coffee since it opened its first shop in 1966, launching the nationwide craft coffee movement and inspiring other chains like Starbucks, Tully's, and others. Peet's had stayed pretty small, with only 201 stand-alone stores, mostly in the West but relatively unknown elsewhere in the country. But in July 2012, it was sold to a private German holding company, Joh. A Benckiser (JAB), for nearly $1 billion.

Even with new ownership, a lot of people are passionately devoted to Peet's coffee and wouldn't think of drinking anything else. Customers and consumers have the same feeling about Apple, Sleep Number Beds, T.J.Maxx, Marshalls, Ritz-Carlton Hotels, Van Bortel Ford in East Rochester, New York, the Taco Bus in Tampa, Florida, and hundreds of other breakout companies.

Why? What are these companies doing that enables them to break out, capture more customers, and create such a loyal connection?

I can tell you this: it's not just years of experience, a quality product, good customer service, or strategic pricing. Here's my answer to this "why" question, based on my years of research and hands-on participation in operating businesses of all sorts: these companies have broken out because they message and deliver solely from their customers' perspective. As a result of sustaining this consumer perspective, their new and existing customers believe these companies have the ability to make a difference in their lives. They have faith in them.

This belief is motivated by different things with different people, but here are some of the leading reasons customers see these companies and others like them as distinct from all others in the marketplace. Customer-centric companies are communicating solely in and from the consumers' point of view. In addition, they not only gain more inquiries but they retain those customers because:

- They know them. The business usually has at least one primary contact who recognizes them when they come in, call, or write.
- They know their taste, their personal style.
- They are their customers' advocates and act as individuals whom customers can trust to look after their particular unique and individual interests.
- They give them a sense of comfort and security. There are no worries about dealing with them and their employees.
- They reduce their customers' stress level, from the simple things like physical strain (not bending over but putting wash in at table-top level) to emotional tension (one-step, perfect choice transactions).
- They liberate them from unnecessary, time-consuming repetition.
- Their product makes them proud. It gives them a special status that provides self-confidence, a sense of themselves to carry forward in their daily life.
- They provide their customers with something they might not know they want until they get it, creating an emotional landing place, a kind of psychological release that gives the customer a warm glow of happiness and accomplishment.

A Story from Early in My Experience

Here's a story about that last reason customer-centric companies don't lose their clients: the emotional landing place, the psychological release.

When I was general sales manager for a Rolls-Royce dealership, I received a call from a well-known celebrity who was looking for a specific Rolls-Royce for his wife's upcoming birthday.

First, I asked him what model he was looking for.

"A Silver Shadow."

"What color?" I asked.

"I know exactly," he replied. "Arctic White with red leather interior and magnolia piping."

"I have that exact model and color in stock," I said, and quoted him the price.

"Sounds about right."

Great! We had exactly what he wanted and the price was right. It was a done deal.

But then something happened. He hesitated. This well-known celebrity — a guy you read about in the papers every day, at the top of his game, even with what I thought were all the pieces in place to close the sale — stopped in his tracks and went silent.

I was puzzled and decided to press ahead.

"Okay," I said finally, unable to bear the silence. "So are we good to go and sign the paperwork?"

No response. Then he kind of mumbled.

"Well, I'm not really sure I want to do this."

Uh-oh!

I was frustrated but felt I had to keep talking. I wasn't going to let this sale slip away for reasons I didn't even understand. So I began to vamp — to improvise and keep the conversation going.

"So where will you and your wife be celebrating?"

He brightened up right away and shared his plans enthusiastically.

"Oh, you know . . . big catered party at our beach house, a hundred people from our A list. Rod Stewart is singing a couple of songs and a few of my comedian friends are doing a kind of gentle spoof tribute to my wife . . ."

"Sounds terrific."

I knew he'd been married for many years now and that this

was a significant birthday. So I kept going, attempting to dig deeper.

"Listen. I know what model and color and price you want, but . . . what else is important to you besides those things? After all, this is a big occasion."

He became quiet again for what seemed like ages, then said, "Well, to be honest with you, I want to give her the Rolls-Royce in a beautiful box."

Aha. Eureka! By asking that last question I had finally reached the jackpot answer, the real feeling he wanted to convey about this present for his wife. The sense of mystery and surprise he wanted to sustain until the very last minute. The level of spectacle opening the box in front of all his guests would provide. The climactic excitement that would deliver that emotional rush and sense of pride.

"So if I build a beautiful box and deliver it to your driveway on her birthday, you'll pay for it?"

"Yes!" he nearly shouted. "Yes. And I don't care what the box costs, if you'll do it."

"Of course. Give me the exact time, date, and address and let's sign the paperwork."

I learned a lot from this experience. A few more buyers over the years went for the beautifully boxed present (when I felt it was the right thing to offer), but more importantly, I learned to keep probing, to pull a potential customer out of a stalled deal by the powerful "what else?" question. To really discover the *why* behind their desire to purchase—the final answer you need to discover the emotional need, the psychological release and fulfillment this purchase really means for the client.

In the years since, we have perfected this process and the language required and taught thousands how to deep-probe with the Power of Why.

Now let's go back to the original challenge we all face when trying to break out in a competitive marketplace.

Back to Basics

When consulting with companies about getting out in front of their competitors in sales volume and market share, we always begin by studying the current operational and customer behavior this business is experiencing. And in most cases, they're back at the stage where their customers and potential customers are still moving from company to company as they search for the best price, incentives, product needs, and customer service. As a result these companies are often offering what is commonly referred to as a Unique Selling Proposition (USP).

A USP represents the conventional, old-fashioned way of increasing sales. It requires constantly jiggering your offer: making small incremental product changes with new models to design and produce, and to persuade people to purchase on a regular basis; constantly changing your price and offering special discounts and incentives in response to other USP style companies; and sleuthing out experimental customer services and perks culled from competitors and business-school consultants, including new leadership styles, team building, and internal motivation.

USP companies focus on themselves and what *they* are doing or how they do things. If sales are flat or declining, they revise their USP because it was a tried-and-true strategy that may have worked for them before.

I have a completely different philosophy. I say you should concentrate on what the *customers* want, what they are doing, and what they want to accomplish. And based on experience, that unique value is information that only the customers can define for us. We can't say what it is until we understand where they're coming from, what their special needs are, and what they want to accomplish by doing business with you.

So our next chapter is going to focus not on the unique *selling* proposition, but rather the *Unique Value Promise* — the process of converting a company that's trying to compete based on unique selling propositions such as company attributes, product features, and price into a company using a customer-centric Unique Value Promise (UVP) focused on emotional meaning, personal benefit, and clear customer outcomes that will capture and keep customers.

This distinction is at the heart of breaking out in a competitive marketplace.

2

What Is the Unique Value Promise?

BEING IN THE MARKETPLACE today is easy, but being found and selected is not.

Regardless of your industry, it's tough to stand out in any marketplace, whether it's local, national, or global. Even if your business is the only one like it, you need a distinctive presence. Without one, you are vulnerable to the first competitor that arrives — and competitors *will* arrive.

Too many businesses think they are distinct because they see themselves as different. Here's why these businesses have to revise their thinking:

1. First and foremost, how a business sees itself or wants to be seen is irrelevant. It's the customer's perspective that matters.
2. Second, and just as important, being different is not the same as having a distinctive presence.

Difference in and of itself is polarizing. Emphasizing what makes a company "different" immediately invites competitive comparisons. Consumers measure and evaluate so-called differences against their other options.

Being truly distinct requires that every facet of your business is consumer-centric. When a business is truly distinctive—by being solely customer-focused—customers flock to it.

In W. Chan Kim and Renée Mauborgne's landmark book *Blue Ocean Strategy*, the authors make a compelling case for having a distinct presence rather than trying to compete head to head. MIT's Sloan School of Management strategy professor Arnoldo Hax has addressed this need to have a distinct presence and customer-centric approach by often repeating the phrase: "Watch our competition, never follow them!"

A business that creates a distinct presence based on the buyer's perspective will be perceived by customers as best in class. Think Starbucks, Nordstrom, Subway, Ross, Ace Hardware, or Southwest Airlines. They are the clear choice in their categories. A business that is customer-centric establishes an emotional bond with its customers, who in turn drive more customers to the business through positive word of mouth—think Whole Foods, Disney, or Victoria's Secret. A business focused solely on its customers and what they want to accomplish is operating with clarity of purpose—a marked change of pace from the constant confusion and chaos caused by working under merchandizing pressure to make the bottom line.

Reaching New Customers and Convincing Them to Buy Is More Difficult Every Day

Consumers have many choices when considering a purchase. Access to competing products and services has never been easier, particularly with the advent of online shopping. The Internet has created another Main Street with many additional stores and providers competing with your business for the same customers. Couple that with the fact that the average individual is constantly told "Buy our product . . . buy from us, because we are good." Whether through online advertising, e-mail tags, radio, TV, newspapers, magazines, or ubiquitous signage, we all endure this constant barrage of business-centric messages and sales calls every day, all day. As a result, consumers have grown disconnected from (and ambivalent about) all but a small number of the messages they hear or see.

Most companies, from the Fortune 50 to mom-and-pop stores, promote their attributes or perceived differences in order to capture the attention of customers and fuel growth. It is a predominant part of the business culture today—an internal focus on who they are, what they have, or how they do things. Many recreational clubs, cultural organizations, and even religious groups follow this same model. As a result, nearly every business, profession, and organization, along with its products and services, has been placed into a commoditized grouping by the consumer. They believe, justifiably, that every business in the market looks, sounds, and likely acts the same.

The Obvious Answer Is Not the Answer

Let's be clear: it doesn't matter that your business has a great name, or that your products and services are unusual or one-of-a-kind. Getting heard and accepted in this noisy, crowded, ever-changing marketplace has never been harder. Buyers today are cautious, skeptical, and solution-driven as never before. They have been burned by the market, misled by politicians, and pushed into a tough financial corner. When customers are deciding to buy, they have one focus: they want to know how doing business with you will be good *for them.*

Every customer asks—long before they engage—"Why should I do business or even inquire with this company? Are they all about themselves or do they actually know and really understand why I want to make a purchase? Most important, will they fulfill what I want and am looking for?" You may assume the answer is obvious. Of course you know why a customer should do business with you! However, you have an understandable bias — your perspective! You think people should do business with you because they want and value things like your:

- good service
- twenty years of experience
- low prices
- large fleet of trucks
- solid warranties
- great selection
- clear communication
- honest approach

The list goes on and on. Every business has its commendable attributes — but they do not engage emotionally with today's buyer. Here's the truth about that, however:

What you do or *who you are* or *how you do it* is not the answer to the question, *Why* should I do business with this company or firm?

Nor do your attributes or features create a distinct presence for your business in the marketplace. They don't answer the *why* question because they don't communicate from the buyer's perspective.

This internal focus on attributes or features as a point of perceived difference is reflected in the advertisements, the so-called branding, business proposals, and promotions all around us. Most businesses are focused on their own perspective as the seller. Most marketing and sales efforts are merchandizing oriented. They focus on products and pricing versus what is needed in today's marketplace: a focus on people and an enduring relationship.

Here is a sampling of the marketing messages that have arrived in my mailbox and e-mail inbox in recent days:

- We provide unique website designs
- We were voted number 1 again
- We are the largest wine wholesaler in the state
- We have the largest selection of affordable furniture in the area
- We were rated best computer service three years in a row

Simply put, they are business- or product-centric, not customer-centric. They convey the qualifications of the company or specifications of the business or its products, but in no way do these messages make them distinct or compel customers to inquire. Sure, this approach worked in the past, but today it reduces perceived value, exacerbates negative perceptions, and invites competitive comparison.

Ironically, all of this commoditization, driven by the wrongheaded merchandizing approach and quest to break out of the crowd, turns a company's focus even more inward. Decisions are made to repackage products and services. It's concluded that a catchy new name or logo is the answer. At the very least, a slick new trendy advertising package is needed to "attract" consumers, all in the pursuit of breaking out and getting them to do business with you.

In today's consumer-centric environment, the value of a business can't be conveyed with an exclusively attribute-centric or offering-centric approach, with rebranding, catchy names, or slick logos.

What Consumers Seek Is Very Different Now

Customers have changed how they decide with whom to do business. They are eagerly seeking out businesses of conviction and purpose. Customers want a business that believes so strongly in what it can provide that it's willing to make a clear, buyer-centric promise of outcome — up front, unconditional, and unqualified.

Make no mistake, this is not the typical brand promise, because the typical brand promise today is a "me"-focused message that neither clarifies value nor delivers distinction.

This desire for a buyer-centric promise is more than the customer wanting to know "what's in it for me" — the classic WIIFM of marketers. Rather, a clear brand promise provides the deep psychological reassurance that a business is committed to customers and is their best choice for what they want to accomplish. This is at the heart of creating a distinct presence in the marketplace and capturing responsive consumers. Responsive consumers are those who have decided to act on their emotional or functional need to solve a problem, fulfill a desire, or make a change.

Thinking you are distinctive is not the same as consumers finding you because you're delivering, at every level of the organization, a consumer-centric promise of outcome in the marketplace. Furthermore, your brand and its promise is not just an image, it's your identity in the marketplace. It provides you with the customer-centric platform needed to break out.

Some years ago I was given a painting commissioned by a CEO client to express his newfound understanding of the consumer's perspective of this point. In black block letters was the word "think," crossed out and replaced by the word "know" in red. The subject — simple; the implications — enormous. Knowing what your target consumers really want and why and delivering it beats what you think every time.

What Is Required to Be Truly Distinct in Today's Competitive Marketplace

Understanding your consumer calls for innovative thinking and a full commitment to a customer-centric focus. I am a huge believer in the future of business, large and small, and believe that anyone can elevate their performance regardless of their present circumstances. However, applying Band-Aids to past strategies and tactics won't work. The pathway to a profitable future requires rethinking and refocusing in the present.

Doing so requires understanding one primary and irrefutable fact: The customer rules!

This rule can't just be given lip service any longer. To paraphrase the late author and philosopher, Jim Rohn, to know, and not to do something about it, is the same as not knowing. Creating a distinct presence by being fully customer-centric requires a deep understanding of what the consumer's perspective truly is, and a commitment to communicate and operate within that perspective relentlessly. It's time to realize that facts trump your perspective.

Focusing solely on the consumer's perspective is not a trend or fad—this is the reality of doing business in today's marketplace. The consumer has reset the paradigm. What worked yesterday is likely wrong today. Unfortunately, many in business have responded to this dramatic shift in the worst possible way by simply continuing to do business in the usual way and hoping for the best.

Creating a distinctive and continual presence requires a deep knowledge and understanding of your customers, both current and prospective. To accomplish this requires a proactive, thorough discovery process to find out why they buy from you, or likely will.

It also requires that every interaction customers have with your organization be positive, personalized, and memorable. Memorable interactions generate positive word of mouth. In today's marketplace, if an attribute-centered ad says, "You will like this," we don't believe it. But if someone says, "I like this," we want to experience it or purchase it ourselves.

Finally, to ensure that your business is truly distinct and sustainable requires a business culture that in and of itself is definable, actionable, and consumer-centric.

Our Own Pathway of Discovery

As a consulting firm, we've had the privilege of helping companies elevate their business performance for many years. Throughout boom times and bust, different strategies and tactics have become appropriate to address different market conditions and changing customer needs. We have dealt with many diverse but related issues, including optimizing organizational structures, elevating service platforms, creating effective marketing campaigns, recruiting the right teams, creating compelling sales presentations, and developing educational programs.

Over the past few years, however, the prevalent issue for new clients has become how to break out of the crowd and drive more inquiries and ultimately more sales. We knew from our discovery process that large marketing expenditures and their often costly rebranding efforts were delivering tepid results. So we decided to systematically analyze a slew of companies that were growing in spite of harsh economic conditions. We wanted to understand what fueled their growth and as a result determine what was missing from other, less effective organizations.

Of the many firms we analyzed, Michelin provides one of the best examples of how developing a unique position and a distinctive presence works in practice. All through the 1970s and 1980s Michelin trailed Goodyear in sales and market share. They had a fantastic reputation for excellence, but they were seen by many as "foreign," "high-end," "expensive," and "for sports cars." Their messaging was very product-centric: "We sell steel-belted radials." But in the 1990s they finally realized the advantage that could be gained by understanding what consumers really wanted and, most important, why.

Yes, customers preferred safe, long-lasting, high-performance steel-belted tires. But Michelin knew that if they could divine *why* those attributes and features were important to the people who bought their tires, they could position themselves from the customer's perspective and become more consumer-centric organizationally.

Michelin sought out their existing customers' input and perspective through extensive market research. Imagine their surprise when their customers revealed the real reason they bought Michelin: they bought Michelin because it was on the cutting edge. Michelin was constantly advancing the technology of tire making, including the raw materials, the process of manufacturing, and standards of security, performance, and durability for the safety and performance of its tires. Armed with this information from their buyers, they crafted a message unique to Michelin, an authentic brand promise of outcome based upon customer input and one that connected emotionally and functionally with them:

"Michelin — a better way forward."

The company then set out to organize every aspect of their sales, service, and organizational culture around their new consumer-centric position and point of distinction so they could break out. Today they promise and deliver "a better way forward." Exactly what consumers want in a tire.

This is not just a slogan. Every part of the organization is constantly seeking to deliver on their brand promise. For instance, like all manufacturers, Michelin offers warranties on their tires — but they offer them as a "promise plan" to achieve a better way forward!

With their relentless focus on the buyer's perspective, Michelin has surpassed Goodyear and its product-centric approach. Goodyear's messaging is all about its tires, relying on so-called brand recognition and unique selling proposition. Goodyear positions itself as it wants to be perceived in the marketplace. Its message is "We are number one in tires!" Really? Nobody cares!

Ask yourself: Why is Michelin winning? The answer is, they are no longer just marketing and selling tires. They are distinct because they are promising and delivering to consumers "a better way forward."

We have discovered in our research that hundreds of forward-thinking businesses have repositioned and reengineered themselves around the consumer perspective. In addition to the national and global firms I mentioned previously are many others, such as Four Seasons Hotels, Morton's The Steakhouse, Wynn Hotel in Las Vegas (even the name has its own sense of customer perspective for those who gamble), and Walmart, and even beloved local firms like Hawaiian Islands Medical in Honolulu, Hawaii. These companies have all created a distinct presence for themselves in their markets by becoming a totally customer-focused enterprise. Consequently, they are outpositioning, outselling, outservicing, and outperforming their competition. From our extensive research we realized that the way to break out in a competitive, commoditized marketplace was to adopt a single-minded focus on the customer's perspective in every area of a business.

The Consequence of Doing Nothing

It's a brave new world out there today. You may have a great business or idea, extraordinary products and services, a legendary brand, even a compelling sales story. But unless you know and understand what consumers really want and why, you'll always wonder why you aren't doing better.

Even the old adage "If you keep doing what you're doing you'll keep getting what you're getting" is no longer true. Keep doing what you're doing these days and you can easily go into a tailspin and not keep getting what you're getting. And it's going to get even tougher going forward. Consumers will only do business with those who position themselves distinctly by understanding, communicating, and consistently delivering the outcomes they seek.

If you're still not convinced of the importance of this idea, look at it another way. When a venture capitalist is offered an opportunity to invest in a firm or an idea, it's high-stakes poker. The initial formal presentation typically makes or breaks the opportunity for all parties involved. The proposal that opens the investor's checkbook is not just about the product or service, or even the leadership.

Venture capitalists assess the potential outcome like every other buyer. They want to know first and foremost what their investment will accomplish for them. They look for the reason this business and its products or services will succeed. What does the consumer want or need, and will this company deliver it? Will that outcome create a distinct presence in the marketplace for this newcomer? Will the promised outcome create a sustainable brand and inspire a corporate team to build an organization to deliver it every day? Ultimately, the answers to questions like these leads to their decision to invest or not.

Understanding the consumer and creating a distinct presence requires diligent execution of the processes revealed in this book. There will be many rewarding milestones to celebrate along the way. Yet never forget that breaking out requires building and keeping a distinct presence by becoming truly consumer-centric. It is an ongoing process, not a singular event. It must become who you are in the marketplace.

ACTION POINTS

1. Ask yourself, is your organization purpose-driven or pressure-driven?
2. Are you constantly competing on price, process, or product features?
3. How many word-of-mouth inquiries are you really receiving each week?

4. As a seller, do you clearly know and understand the buyer's perspective? More importantly, are you solely focused on delivering to it?

5. Does your target customer see your business as set apart from all other providers?

3

How Consumers Define and Respond to Your Unique Value Promise

ANY CEO, SALES, AND MARKETING executives assume that all their customers really want is a low price or a "bargain." But, from our extensive experience interviewing hundreds of buyers at every economic level in many industries, this is emphatically not true.

This is why a step-by-step, mission-specific discovery process is so vital for your success in getting way out in front of the pack. Asking your best customers the right questions in the right way will get you to the very core of what buyers actually accomplish, both functionally and emotionally, by doing business with you. You'll clearly see the "why" behind what they say they value and prefer. You'll discover from your best customers what they really want and need at a deep level and how they are or are not receiving it from your business.

Your Unique Value Promise, crafted from this single-focus discovery effort, will create consumer curiosity and new potential buyer responsiveness. Here's a brief, unsolicited perspective from one of the best salespeople in an organization that used one of our scripted questionnaires for this purpose with her clients:

"Until I did my first interview, I had been looking at this undertaking with jaded skepticism. What I found out right away, however, was that this seemingly innocuous eighteen-question survey gave me a window into the inner workings of my top clients' reasons for being with me and, most importantly, why! In their answers, always truthful and difficult to formulate, they found an opportunity they'd never had before: to tell me what they really thought of me and what our company really helped them accomplish. As if that weren't enough, it also uncovered and paved the way for additional opportunities to service them."

The Difficulty of Change

Change can be tough for anyone, especially a business organization that's been doing things the same way for a long time. Nevertheless, so many such companies these days want to break out in an increasingly competitive marketplace.

To do so, you must be willing to abandon your old offer-centric perspective. You and those people on your team who assist with this process must surrender your point of view and wholly commit to uncovering the point of view of your best customers to create a distinctive presence in a commoditized, competitive marketplace; a position so distinctive it will elevate your entire organization's business performance. This isn't easy. It requires self-discipline and no self-indulgence. Know that many have made this shift and commitment successfully. You and your team can do it, too—once your purpose is clear.

The first thing that must occur for this effort to be successful is to reconcile in your mind that it is okay to ask for help.

Our experience with many company executives shows that the very idea of asking anyone for input, even their best customers, is disturbing. We've heard plenty of arguments why interviewing customers to find a Unique Value Promise is unusual or, at the very least, not "normal."

We hear everything from "We don't want to look like we don't know what we are doing" to "We already know why they buy."

My team has had a lot of experience overcoming this kind of mind-set. Sometimes we start out with King Solomon's proverb, "Before honor comes humility."

This advice is essential. We urge those working through this discovery process to approach their top customers with humility and empathy—and most do. They learn to embrace the expectation that they'll capture fresh insight that will fuel profits and growth.

Deep Discovery Is More Than a Cursory Process

It follows then that the discovery process itself be more than cursory. I'll detail the mechanics of the process further along in this book. However, keep in mind that it's essential that this process be done with one customer at a time, face-to-face, as a stand-alone interaction, with no other items to discuss but this deep discovery. A social setting like breakfast, lunch, or over coffee or tea is ideal and forty to forty-five minutes or so is all the time required for each best-customer interview. The important overriding principle is to personalize and humanize the interview experience. Only when you personalize and humanize will your customers engage openly and reveal the real, deep-seated reasons for why they do business with you.

This *is not* a focus group exercise. Getting deep functional and emotional discovery cannot be done in a group setting. Focus groups have their place; this is not it.

We have also learned that a telephone call has nowhere near the same discovery outcome as a face-to-face interaction. We've had clients whose best customers are half a world away so they've learned to use Skype quite effectively. I recommend this only if the setup on each end is private and conducive to open interaction and deep discovery.

Without a solid foundation, the distinct presence needed to

break out cannot be achieved. The foundation of distinctiveness is not the same as your vision or mission statement. As our senior vice president Dick Harris is fond of saying, "Vision is the *what* and the *when* of the process." I'd add that your mission statement is the *how*. But the what, when, and how of what you do is not the answer. The foundation of a distinct presence is a rock-solid understanding of the *real* reason why people buy from you. It's knowing and communicating the real functional and emotional outcome buyers achieve through your business and its products and services.

What Do Consumers Seek in Your Promise?

When deciding with whom to do business, buyers review print and online media for the business that can offer the results they want. They ask family, friends, and acquaintances, "What has this business or product done for you?" Or they ask, "Who do you know that can help me with . . ." and then they articulate what they really want to achieve and, most critically, why! They know that by asking other customers they will get an honest, consumer-centric perspective. Here are some examples:

- "I'm tired of the same haircut and I want a new look— who's your hairstylist?"
- "I want to buy a more reliable car—what have you heard about this particular make and model?"

Every one of us thinks this way.

Ask yourself, why are you really on Facebook? You may say because it's cool or easy or fun, but the real reason why is likely to be "To stay connected to friends and family."

Or, why did you switch banks? Perhaps the first answer is, "Because they are open late." But the real reason why is the outcome: They make it easier to get your banking done within your schedule.

Or, why did you buy a bigger boat? Your first answer could be, "I wanted to cruise even in rough water." But the real reason why is that you wanted to get out on the water whenever you pleased.

Why purchase an extended warranty? Worry-free ownership. That's a truly compelling outcome.

Without understanding the real reason why people buy, you miss the opportunity to be customer-centric and distinct. No one buys anything or even inquires unless they feel a business can help them accomplish what they really want. They don't just want to buy a new home or put in a new yard or buy a new motorcycle or send their child to a certain college. No, they have a deep-seated reason why—a specific, powerful outcome they want to achieve.

Consumers today want a Unique Value Promise crafted solely from their perspective, and they know the difference between a promise and a proposition. A Unique Value Promise does exactly what the words say—it creates a unique brand promise of value for the consumer. Crafted properly, it is authentic to your business and nearly impossible for competitors to duplicate, thus adding to your distinct presence. A Unique Value Promise is one that compels the consumer to inquire because of the functional applications and emotional benefits it holds for them. Void of any reference to the attributes and features of your business, it's delivered solely from the consumer's perspective.

Your Promise Makes You Distinct

Because it's completely customer-centric, your Unique Value Promise, crafted with best-customer input, will not only compel other consumers to inquire, it will make your business stand out in the marketplace. You'll switch the focus from being *different* to being *unique*. For one thing, you'll communicate truly from the buyer's perspective; for another, your promise will be authentic to you and to what you actually deliver every day.

Think about companies that make an authentic Unique Value Promise and consistently deliver it both externally and internally. In addition to all those I have already mentioned, think Sports Authority, Bass Pro Shops, Hatteras, or Top-Flite. Their UVP—and its relentless delivery at every level of their organizations—has made them distinct and as a result they are breakout companies. They are not just competing; their names are synonymous with what people will actually accomplish by doing business with them. Moreover, they know that the consistent delivery on their brand promise is what enables them to keep their distinctive position with consumers.

A clear, uncompromising promise of value positions you in the mind of the consumer. People love to tell the story of what they accomplished working with a remarkable business, whether it's how they booked a great trip, got their house painted, or even got a great haircut. Their positive word of mouth will move others into your pipeline. That buzz, that referral flow, combined with the relentless promotion and consistent delivery of your UVP, will set your company and its products apart from all others.

How Customers React to a Unique Value Promise

Articulating what customers want to experience or accomplish with a Unique Value Promise generates two reactions that compel customers to respond.

First, "Wow! Really?"

Many customers experience sheer disbelief when a business touches the very core psychological reasons for their desire to buy. It's actually very unusual for a business to understand what its customers want to accomplish and *why*, so that when one does, customers feel as though all their psychological needs are encapsulated in a UVP. Consequently, if your UVP is solid and consistent, they'll feel as though you are on their side—and thus that their business belongs with you.

After surprise comes curiosity. The right UVP will inspire customers to inquire. The question that your brand promise must create in a potential customer's mind when they see it or hear it is, "How do they do that?" This only happens, however, if the value promised does in fact convey a real functional and emotional outcome and is crafted solely in their words and from their point of view. But if *your* perspective seeps into your promise, customers will see it as just another old-school selling proposition and business-centric statement.

Another advantage of a compelling, relevant Unique Value Promise is that it creates distinction even in conversation. It changes how you and everyone in your organization responds to the age-old question, "What do you do?"

In company- and product-centric organizations, the normal response to this question by owners, executives, and sales, service, and marketing types is a fifteen-second "elevator speech," typically all about them. For example, "Our company has been in business for fifteen years. We sell and service a wide range of computer printers, including Canon, HP, Xerox, and Epson." Or, "Our real estate firm has a proven sales track record. We give our clients personalized service and have a large inventory of properties at all times." Neither of these examples says anything about what customers will accomplish with the company.

Your Unique Value Promise replaces the old and obsolete elevator speech. When you and your team are asked what you do for a living, respond with your UVP. It will immediately set you apart. Here are two examples: "I work for a consulting company that elevates business performance in today's marketplace." Or, "Our software support firm improves our clients' productivity and reduces their downtime."

Responding with your brand's promise of value when asked "What do you do?" almost always compels people to ask, "How?"

Of course, not every interaction will lead to a business opportunity, nor should it. But using your Unique Value Promise to articulate what you do for people will make you memorable and distinctive every time.

Doesn't Brand Equity Count?

I'm often asked by our new clients, "What about our brand equity? Doesn't our brand recognition set us apart? Don't the highlighted attributes of our business and our products or services within our brand promise generate ongoing sales and loyalty?"

My answer is that, alas, even though brand equity can be a very valuable asset, it in no way ensures continued success in this consumer-driven marketplace.

There is a long list of local, regional, and national businesses with brand equity that have struggled or failed in the past several years. Vast amounts of time, effort, and capital go into tweaking marketing messages, merchandising processes, and sales presentations, all to leverage brand equity. Most companies have relied on the traditional four Ps — products, place, price, and promotion — to leverage brand equity or business-centric brand messages to maintain velocity. Some have even adopted three additional Ps as a way to cope: people, process, and physical evidence.

Yet even with these keys in place, consumers are still confused, reluctant to inquire, and hesitant to buy. Why? They want a reason to inquire. Consequently, the need for an eighth P is essential: *promise.* Consumers want a functional and emotional brand promise of outcome — from *their* perspective, not yours — that addresses clearly and solely why they want to buy. Any part of the message that carries your perspective, even in nuance, risks being perceived as a business-centric sales pitch.

When customers learn about your brand promise, they'll feel confident about the results they will get by doing business with you. If it's delivered consistently, they'll see your UVP as your doctrine, your policy regarding what your business will do for customers like them time and time again. It inspires trust and confidence. Ultimately, it becomes what you are known for in your market space and sets you apart from all others.

Instead of talking about your business or products, which results in further commoditization, you are talking about what consumers achieve by buying from you. The result? Buyers will repeat your Unique Value Promise to friends, family, and colleagues. They will take pride in the fact that they made a good choice, and will want to pass it on. When you consistently deliver on your promise, they aren't just satisfied customers. They are delighted advocates—thrilled at what doing business with you has accomplished for them. As a result, they will push more buyers to you.

What Other Forward-Thinking Firms Use Unique Value Promises?

As mentioned previously, companies of all sizes have embraced this strategy. They are making brand promises unique to them and, as a result, experiencing great consumer responsiveness and growth in spite of dire economic conditions.

Here are a few I admire:

ING U.S. Financial Services — "We Make It Easy for You"

This Dutch-based financial company understands that in the complex, confusing world of insurance and finance, a promise of simplicity will create curiosity in the frustrated consumer. "Finally," consumers think to themselves, "here is someone who realizes how confusing it all is and wants to make it easy for me! How can they help me?"

Google — "Organizing the World's Information and Making It Universally Accessible and Useful"

Everybody knows Google is synonymous with Internet searching. They are the iconic brand in that space. Their name has become a widely accepted verb, as in "I'll Google that." But how did they get there? Since starting in 1996, when the founders built their first search engine (called "Backrub"), Google has stayed relentlessly true to their promise to consumers. Today Google is not just a search engine—their skill at organizing information in arenas ranging from scholarly research to e-mail has made them even more distinct. They are the creators of the new Main Street of the World.

FedEx— "When Your Package Absolutely, Positively Has to Get There Overnight"

FedEx was founded on the idea that people needed fast air-freight delivery. But the company subsequently dug down to discover the real reason why people were using their service. They found that customers used them because it was essential that their package be delivered overnight. Result: FedEx promises this, delivers it, and is the dominant firm in overnight courier service worldwide.

At this point, you may be thinking that only large businesses with big marketing dollars can afford the research to find out why people buy from them. In reality, many large businesses got that way because they understood early on what people wanted to accomplish and why. Consequently, they created a distinct presence in the marketplace and grew very quickly.

Let's look at a few examples of midsize and even smaller firms that are positioned appropriately to become iconic brands.

Olive Garden — "When You're Here, You're Family"

This chain makes a great promise. Perfect for those who want to feel as though they can be themselves while dining out—casual, no dressing up, not feeling as if they have to keep up with the Joneses. And great for those wondering whether they should really take the kids. Yes, you may want Italian food because it is a true comfort food. But part of comfort is being with, and being treated like, family! People say, "Hmm, do they really treat us like family? Let's go find out."

Dollar General — "Save time. Save money. Every day!"

Any store with "dollar" in its name shouldn't have to worry about getting customers to see the value, right? Not Dollar General — they leave nothing, and I mean nothing, to chance. Their promise has allowed them to break out in targeted markets even with the "low prices every day" value promise of Walmart. How? With a functional *and* emotional promise. Who doesn't want to save money *and* time, every day? That's an outcome ideally suited to our hectic, tight-budget world.

Insperity — "Inspiring Business Performance"

This midsize consulting firm offers a compelling and distinctive reason to do business with them. For twenty-five years they have delivered employment, recruiting, and retirement services to companies of different sizes. Yet they get your attention with their well-articulated promise before they get into how they do it! The more you think about this, the more you realize that everyone wants their employees to feel inspired. Which leads to, "How can they do that for my business?"

Lifelock — "Relentlessly Protecting Your Identity"

This identity-theft protection firm has many different levels of services and lots of notification processes to alert you if someone attempts to steal your identity. They could go on ad nauseam about how they do it. Instead, their Unique Value Promise says it all. The first thought a potential customer has is, "How do they do that?" Given what a huge issue this is — and one that is frequently in the news — the next step people take is to inquire and find out the details.

La-Z-Boy — "Live Life Comfortably"

This company makes certain every one of its many product offerings constantly reinforces this message. They are very consistent in promoting their promise, keeping it front and center in all their messaging and company interactions. In a recent ad, when asked her view of a recliner, spokesperson Brooke Shields says, "This is a La-Z-Boy? Pinch me! (Actually, don't pinch me; I'm too comfortable right now.)" No wonder they thrive even in stressful times.

Pella — "We Help You Turn Your Vision Into Reality"

Specializing in windows and doors for new homes as well as the replacement market, Pella's promise delivers on different levels. Even when new home construction is at a near standstill, their promise enables them to continue to grow and be profitable in the replacement market.

Even at the small business level, there are successful examples of a customer-centric philosophy:

Pacific Medical Healthcare & Supply — "Making Life Easier"

This single store is packed with every type of medical device you can imagine. They carry twenty-two different product lines, from communication aids to orthopedic support. However, not a word of that is in their Unique Value Promise. Anyone who needs medical and health-care supplies obviously wants to find *the* store that can help them make life easier. Even though they are in a back street in a warehouse district and pricing is retail, their traffic looks more like wholesale.

Even artists need a promise, and some get it right. For instance, Neal Borowsky, aka "Steel Neal," who started out as a poet, is best known for his incredible *Agony of Man* sculpture. Steel Neal creates his art from found items such as I-beams and New York City garbage cans. But he doesn't just rely on what collectors and critics said they valued about his art—his use of steel and his talent to craft it with style. Instead, he creates "Art That Saves the World." His Unique Value Promise positions his business and talent distinctly.

Customer-centric companies communicate and are deeply committed to their brand promise, which is solely focused on customer outcome. They know it sets them apart. They don't talk about their products and services or expertise or perceived dominance, with expressions like "We are number one!" They don't talk about who they are or how they do things. Instead, in every way possible they talk about what they will do for the consumer solely from the buyer's perspective. Following this path of declaring value and outcome from the buyer's perspective creates definitive consumer responsiveness that begins with curiosity. And this curiosity leads to inquiries, and ultimately to purchases. As a result, these companies are winning new customers who were likely another company's loyalty-neutral "satisfied" customers "willing to explore other options."

Strategically, a customer-centric UVP is not just a nice sentiment. It's essential to connecting the dots, removing uncertainty, and clarifying value from the consumer's perspective. It captures consumer interest by speaking directly to what today's buyers crave. Most important, it enables any business to establish a unique position in their marketplace and separate themselves from the competition. Ultimately, what this means for your business is more consumer inquiries and more sales.

When you uncover your Unique Value Promise, it becomes the central purpose and passion of your enterprise. It influences all your go-to-market activities, including messaging, new products, pricing, distribution, sales, ongoing service, and even physical locations. Fully integrating your UVP puts your entire team on purpose and also determines the type of employees you hire.

Do you have a UVP that represents an authentic brand promise of real outcome for the customer? Is it crafted with direct best-customer input? Does it speak clearly to what they desire to accomplish, and why? The power of really knowing *why* people do business with you trumps every other perspective, including yours. What you do is good, no doubt. But communicating and delivering what buyers truly crave every time is invaluable. It establishes you firmly in your market as the best, and being the best is priceless. Your brand promise, uncovered from your best customers and crafted with care, will be the foundation on which you establish your distinct presence. It will allow you to break out in a competitive marketplace.

ACTION POINTS

Write out your one-sentence answer to the question, "Why should I do business with you?" Then ask yourself:

1. Does your answer capture the prospect's attention by addressing what they really want to accomplish?
2. Does it position you as distinct in the marketplace? Specifically, would your competitors be likely to give the same answer you did?
3. Is any part of it about you and your business (your perspective) or is it solely about what consumers can really accomplish (from their perspective) and why that's important to them?
4. Is it about convincing prospects to buy or does it speak clearly to a promise that provides the deep functional and emotional outcomes they seek?

Part II

SIX STEPS TO BREAKING OUT IN A COMPETITIVE MARKETPLACE

4

Step One: The Rules of Engagement

E'VE SEEN THE IMPORTANCE of letting your customers help define your company's Unique Value Promise. This requires deep research, beyond the level most of us have conducted up to this point. This is not something, moreover, that you can farm out to an ad agency or the research department or even just to the marketing department. Yes, there are ways to use their expertise in preparation for this research, like studying this book and creating interview questions following the guidelines detailed herein. But having done that, you and your customer-facing team will have to roll up your sleeves and do the actual best- customer interviews. There's no getting away from it.

To be sure your selected customer-facing team gets this right, be sure to educate them on the importance of the process. Explain that their efforts will be critical to establishing a distinct presence for your business in the marketplace and helping you break out. Have them read and then discuss this entire book as a team before beginning to approach the best-clients research.

I'll be laying down some strong advice for the process that follows, but even before you start reading, let me reiterate that under no circumstances should anyone except customer-facing sales or service personnel conduct these interviews. Only they have the proven ability to put the customer at ease and find the "why" and "what" for the building blocks for your UVP!

Enough said by way of introduction. Now let's plunge into the nitty-gritty, the best practices I've developed from years of consultation and experience in the field, what I call the rules of engagement for having your customers define your company's Unique Value Promise.

Rule of Engagement #1

Select the customers from whom you want input wisely.

Choose only those who are the best customers of your business and its products or services. These best customers are clearly aware of the functional advantages and emotional benefits they receive by doing business with you. They are certain, beyond any doubt, that you are the best and only provider for them. With this in mind, ask yourself the following questions:

- Who has a relationship at a deep level with your sales and service organization?
- Who are the consistent users of your products or services?
- Who is it that always recommends or refers other people to you?

These are the customers who want to see you continue to grow, succeed, and win.

These individuals, moreover, are the types of people you want more of as you grow your business.

He or she may be the executive who continually uses your raw materials and makes the purchase decisions. Or the engineer who consistently recommends your hot water heaters or boilers in his/her design specs. Or the office manager who always calls you for all his printing needs or copier repairs or even office cleaning. She could be one of your frequent shoppers or service users of your business.

These best customers will be the source of greatest input. They have a very clear perspective about why they do business with you continually and will provide the input and specific words needed to craft your Unique Value Promise. They have an emotional bond with you and your company. If you are a small business, selecting eight to ten of these best customers will give you all the input you need to find your way to a compelling UVP. Larger businesses (even Fortune 50) need to sample no more than one hundred of their very best customers to find the insight they need.

Choose your interviewees wisely. If you have multiple product lines or a large footprint, avoid choosing from only one user group or area. Get input, as Greg Ostergren did at American National (as reported in his foreword to this book), from customers using various products in a wide geographic area to insure an authentic UVP for the business.

If you are engaged in a start-up, choose those prospects who are likely potential customers. They may live in the geographic area where you intend to open your business. Or they may already be involved in the industry in which you will sell your product or service. In every case, be sure to talk with individuals who are clearly potential purchasers.

Opening a restaurant? Who goes out to dinner frequently in your area? Talk with them. Lawn care? Who has some of the best-kept lawns in your area? Opening a garden shop or nursery? Talk to the master gardeners in your area, and the flower club. Clear thought and good research prior to selecting those you will interview ensures you will talk to the right people and that you'll get the right perspective.

Rule of Engagement #2

Create and use a mission-specific questionnaire with preset questions.

Current customer-satisfaction surveys or focus group question-naires you may have on hand or that you've used before are not appropriate tools here. What's needed is a series of prepared questions specific to this discovery.

This is critical and affords many advantages. You guarantee that by interviewing your best customers with the same mission-specific right questions you'll have the ability to analyze their varied responses. It also ensures that the interviewers have a track and a process to follow. This allows them to not only ask different customers the same questions but also, with prepared questions, to probe deeply. Deep probing is essential. You want the deep-seated functional and emotional reasons *why* your best customers say what they value and prefer from your company and what is important to them.

Your questionnaire should ask not just four or five but fifteen to eighteen specific questions about your company, sales process, and services. As an example, you might ask, What do you believe are our three greatest strengths as a company? Follow that question with, Why are these strengths important to you? Another could be, How would you rate our customer service—excellent, good, fair? Then ask, Why did you rate it that way?

Your series of *why* questions should be interspersed with two or three product and service awareness questions. Find out what they know about the other products and services you provide. In addition, use this process to gain their perspective regarding the advantages of your products or services they are using. List six to seven of them, and as you read each of them, ask:

What does this feature or attribute actually accomplish for you?

What important benefit does that provide for you?

These questions about your offerings' features, when explored, answered, and preserved verbatim, will be pure gold when you integrate them into your sales processes and responses to their inquiries. I'll detail more about exactly how they're used in Chapter 8.

For example, I remember when Toyota first introduced the

Lexus into the United States in 1989. As a young man, I was curious about this new entry and brand. Incidentally, Toyota rightly
realized that the affluent were not going to pay $30,000 to $45,000
(and now much more) for a vehicle marketed in Japan as a Toyota
Celsior. Thus, Lexus was born! In my first encounter with Lexus,
I visited the newly constructed showroom and was greeted by a
friendly, smiling salesperson. He immediately asked me two very
key questions — first, "Why do you want to buy a Lexus?" and after
I answered, he asked, "Whom do you want to buy it for?"

Therein, I believe, was the catalyst for the explosive acceptance
and growth of Lexus. Their entire national sales force was taught
to ask these questions. By asking left- and right-brain questions
they immediately had a clear understanding of why people inquired and what they wanted to accomplish. The same occasional
insertion of left-brain questions is powerful in the UVP discovery
process as well.

Be sure each interview ends with a gracious thank-you and a
clear request for (and commitment to) more input. These words
placed at the end of the questionnaire and articulated clearly by
the interviewer sets the stage for the next step with them:

"I'll be coming back to you so we can share what I believe are
our several potential Unique Value Promises for customers like
you and ask you to help us select the right one! Fair enough?"
Wow — do they glow when they hear that! Also, don't worry about
some questions being too personal or too detailed. Our experience
with our firm's proprietary best-customer survey shows that customers are comfortable with all the questions.

It is the interviewer who is often uncomfortable because he or
she doesn't know the answers in advance. The sole objective is to
find out what the customers value and prefer, and most importantly, why.

Finally, be very careful that the discovery questions you create
in no way steer people to answers that reinforce *your* perspective.
This process has one objective — their perspective!

Rule of Engagement #3

Interview your selected individuals face-to-face.

It's essential to reinforce this point. Mailing questionnaires will give you useless responses and will actually hurt this initiative.

We recently worked with a firm whose CEO was very much an alpha personality. At first, he agreed with and understood the need for face-to-face interviewing. Later, however, he decided he could "save time and money" by mailing out the surveys we created for his firm instead of conducting face-to-face interviews. It didn't matter that we'd discussed and explained the importance of this rule of engagement in detail. He mailed them anyway.

Only nine of the twenty-four mailed surveys were returned. Only two had more than a few words as answers to any of the questions. Not one of the nine returned answered the deeper probing questions. As a result, zero—absolutely nothing of what the customers said—was important or useful. Thus the company lost money, valuable time, and the irreplaceable opportunity to conduct these surveys face-to-face with some of their very best customers.

Some, unfortunately, are destined to learn the hard way, through their own mistakes and not through experienced consultation and education.

And as I mentioned previously, calling customers on the telephone doesn't work. You won't be able to see their body language or facial expressions as they respond. Nor can they see yours. This is a real disadvantage as you work at probing deeply and getting to their "why." Also as noted earlier, technology such as Skype, which allows you to see and visually interact with the customer, can work, but only if the setting is congenial, comfortable, confidential, and allows for candid interaction.

Now you might be thinking that a retail store can't really make this face-to-face interaction work. But it can! Most loyal customers have a salesperson they like to deal with when they shop your store. They feel comfortable with them and have a sense that that salesperson knows what they like. Use this knowledge to your advantage! Have that salesperson invite his or her loyal customer to breakfast, lunch, or to have midday coffee or tea. No matter what type of business you have, it's magical when you ask for help.

Rule of Engagement #4

Use only your client/customer-facing team to conduct the face-to-face interviews.

This initiative works brilliantly only when those who have the relationship with the customer engage them. Knowledge and trust are built face-to-face. The sales rep, the client manager, the marketing or service rep who continually interacts with these best customers has a special relationship with them. They'll have little to no reluctance in sharing their deep feelings with their reps. Face-to-face interviews by your customer-facing team ultimately provides the rapport and chemistry needed to get full, transparent answers. In contrast, delegating the discovery portion of this process to the marketing or PR department, your advertising firm, or some other committee will reduce the quality level of the responses you seek.

As mentioned earlier in this chapter, it's possible that a select team from marketing, advertising, or public relations, if you have them, can help prepare the best-customer mission-specific questionnaire. This select team can also tabulate the responses. They may even help craft possible UVPs based on the best customers' words and responses. But under no circumstances should anyone except customer-facing sales or service personnel conduct these interviews. Only they have the proven ability to put the customer at ease, discover their why, and assemble the building blocks for your UVP!

Rule of Engagement #5

Use a well-thought-out, rehearsed approach to position the interview correctly.

Everyone is busy. Engaging individual best customers for forty to forty-five minutes requires tact and sensitivity. Our experience has shown that interviewees will agree to participate only if you ask them in a way that makes them feel important. Your request, positioned and approached correctly, gives them the psychological sense of recognition and the exhilaration of a new experience.

Asking correctly also makes them feel meaningful and significant—a fundamental psychological need of every human. The actual scripting to set the appointment for the interview can vary depending on your type of business and style:

"We're repositioning and rebranding our business and want to be sure we get our best customers' input. We need forty to forty-five minutes with you over breakfast or lunch to get your insight and advice."

"You are one of our best customers and we are always striving to be better at what we offer. That's why your opinion is important to us. So let's have breakfast or lunch one day next week so I can get your insight and advice. Would Tuesday or Thursday be best?"

"We're starting a business in the area and want to be sure we get the insight from people we feel are in the know. We think that is you and we are looking for forty-five minutes to meet with you to seek any advice you can give us."

The key is to acknowledge them and position the value of their input. These invitations should be made verbally, either in person or over the phone with a warm, relational tone. Two important things we have learned *not to do* when inviting:

- Don't send a written invitation to participate. It requires too much explanation and doesn't have the same immediate connection as a warmly spoken overture.

- Beware of telling them you want to find out "why they do business with you" when you extend the invitation. This nearly always brings the same response: "Oh, we don't have to meet—you know why!" and then you nearly always get a perfunctory, off the top of their head, generic values or preferences statement. Statements such as "Because you give good service," or "You are the best," or some other bland response—one that you now know is useless in uncovering the Power of Why for your UVP.

Position your discovery as outlined above. Make the request, get a response (which will nearly always be yes), and schedule a convenient time. That's it! Save further defining of the process until you meet with them face-to-face.

Oh—and be sure you rehearse the invitation script out loud before you use it, so you say it like you own it. If you rehearse it out loud several times, you *will* own it!

Rule of Engagement #6

The setting sets the tone.

Remember, this is an engaging conversation, not a third-degree investigation. So adjust your mind-set and focus on creating a friendly partnership experience.

Choose a quiet setting where you can talk and hear well, a location where your interviewee can feel comfortable sharing their deep thoughts and feelings, and you can capture their answers as you converse. That's why a setting like breakfast or lunch in a quiet place works so well. It creates a social atmosphere where people will naturally relax.

Rule of Engagement #7

Listen actively and capture responses verbatim.

Taking the time and trouble to write down exactly what your customer says is one of the essential keys to discovering the actual building blocks to a compelling customer-centric UVP.

Customers express themselves from their point of view. It's the only perspective they know. And you'll find out very quickly that their view is much different from yours. When asked to explain what you do for them, and with probing to discover why they answered the way they did, their perspective will pour forth. With the right questions they'll illustrate their perspective with lively language, painting word pictures, even using graphic illustrations to be sure you understand what they really accomplish with your company, products, or services and most importantly why it is important to them.

They will uncover both the functional and the emotional reasons in actual words that are beyond valuable—they're priceless. People want to talk, explain, characterize why they are your best customers. Or, in the case of a start-up, they'll want to detail the emotional and functional reasons why they'd buy from you. For this reason it is absolutely vital that the specific words and phrases of those interviewed be captured verbatim.

So slow down, ask them to repeat anything you didn't catch, listen again, and write out their answers. They will be patient and wait. They'll be flattered that you are paying such close attention and that you want to capture their words and phrases precisely.

It's also important that you read the questions aloud. We heard from one seller who let his best clients read the questions themselves over lunch and fill in their responses. "I didn't want to have to write them myself. But maybe I made a mistake. They didn't really reveal that much."

Discovery only works when every question is read to them directly from the questionnaire and their word-for-word responses are captured verbatim. Having the questions read to them makes the interviewee more thoughtful and emphasizes the importance of the process. Further, no questions are skipped or missed.

Avoid using any technology during these interviews. We've discovered that many see laptops or tablets as an intrusion, regardless of the age of the person interviewed. Also, tape or digital recorders, from our experience, chill the conversation. These devices tend to elicit guarded replies to most questions.

We've heard many excuses about why writing down word for word what customers say is a real problem. None are valid. This is not about what's easy for you or your team. It's about what puts the client at ease and allows them to open up.

Finally, remember these are one-on-one, face-to-face discussions with your best customers, *not* two-on-one with an assistant present to take good notes. Instead, listen fast and write slow.

Rule of Engagement #8

Spreadsheet their answers.

The excitement you'll experience at the conclusion of your best-customer interviewing process will be palpable. Your customer will be elated by the experience. Those who've conducted the interview will be thrilled to have gotten several "aha's" and a great sense of satisfaction.

The next step is to select an individual in your organization who is detail oriented and able to create a spreadsheet detailing each survey question and the actual answers of all participants. This will allow you and others to compare the different same-question responses, identifying clear themes, phrases, and descriptive words.

The insight gained from this spreadsheeting is inspiring and you will find it in some ways shocking. It's inspiring because it shows how clearly customers articulate what they really accomplish through your business and, most significantly, why it is important to them. It's shocking because it shows how differently they see your business and its offerings. But remember, their perspective is not the same as yours.

Having had the pleasure of reading literally hundreds of surveys conducted by our clients, I never cease to be amazed at the responses. Here are just a few examples of some clear customer reasons why they chose and continue to do business with various companies (extracted from a number of best-customer surveys):

Their answers relating to questions about what the company did for them (e.g., what they valued and preferred)	Deep Probe Responses to WHY is that important	
	Functional Advantage	Emotional Benefit
Clear plan	Helps me prioritize	So I am more productive
Good counsel	Consistently gives me the information I need	So I make good decisions
Casual relaxed dining	Always have a fun, relaxing evening	Makes eating out more enjoyable
Quiet rooms	I get a good night's sleep	Keeps me effective when I travel
Fully equipped gym	Gives me a great workout	I feel better about myself
Proactive design services	Shows me creative ways to solve engineering issues	We deliver a great plan
Low-cost printing	It keeps my printing costs within budget	You help me make a profit!
Years of experience	I find great insight to help me make decisions	I hate making mistakes
FAST delivery	You get our goods to market on time	It helps me keep my customers
Personal shopper experience	You always help me find the right "look"	I want to always look my best!

As you read through your spreadsheet of answers to each question, be open to new thoughts, phrases, concepts, and language. It will be their perspective, their real "why," and it may look and sound very different from anything you've heard or thought of before. Be prepared to receive it. It is how your best customers see your business — from their perspective.

Now we're ready to take the results of these interviews and go on to the next step in creating your Unique Value Promise.

5

Step Two: Crafting Your Promise

F ROM HERE ON WE need to tread carefully, and not alone. It's best if you select a group of three to four (not ten to fifteen) individuals in your organization whom you can rely on to craft your UVP from the customers' responses. Or, if you are a very small business or a start-up, use three to four of your advisers and mentors.

As with the team that conducted the interviews originally, have them all read and discuss this entire book before starting out. Don't just brief—educate them and discuss with them the outcome needed prior to commencement. They each need to understand that the purpose of the process and the desired outcome is to uncover and craft your Unique Value Promise using your best customers' words only.

Be sure that the individuals you choose have the characteristics found in this checklist:

- They should be creative and able to think outside the box.
- They need to be willing and able to set aside their own opinions, perspectives, and personal agendas.
- They need to be able to work both independently and as a team.

The Team Process Begins with Each Crafter Working Alone

At first, each crafter needs to work independently, delving deeply only into the "why" portions of the response spreadsheet.

During this solitary period, each should look for and highlight repeated or common word usage and phraseology, including nouns, verbs, adjectives, and adverbs, both formal and vernacular. The crafters' job at this point is to extract all the functional and emotional language that your best customers used to illustrate why they do business with you. It is from these actual words and phrases that your UVP will evolve, not modified into your words, but using only the customers' words and perspectives.

Their next step is to draft potential language for the Unique Value Promise, plugging and unplugging the customers' exact "why" words and phrases. Each potential UVP must have a functional component (think "what it does") and an emotional component (think "the benefit to the customer"). The order isn't important. Including both, however, is!

Each potential UVP candidate must represent only the customers' perspective. The crafters shouldn't take on or insert their own language to provide perspective "for clarity." Rather, they should craft a UVP that prompts the curiosity question from prospective buyers: "How do they do that?"

The objective is for each team member to develop two to three possible UVPs on their own, each consisting of four to eight words. Fewer than four can be a bit too pithy and create more consumer confusion than curiosity. More than eight usually creates too much story and not enough curiosity to inquire.

The goal of a UVP is to motivate, not fully educate!

UVP Team Collaboration Commences

When each team member has crafted two or three draft UVPs, the team can meet to discuss each member's candidates. They should then brainstorm, combine, reject, modify, mix words and phrases, and graft from their individual potential UVPs. No problem. But they cannot craft choices based upon what they *think* people meant. They must remain true to your best customers' actual "why" responses.

The end result of this crafting exercise is to agree on three to four solid final choices as a team. To provide your team guidance, here are some of the "why" answers that could appear on a best-customer survey and how they can be assembled into a UVP.

A financial firm's "why" portion of their survey spreadsheet might say:

"You make things simple for us."

"You clarify the complex financial things in our life."

"You really simplify our financial decisions."

"You make investing so simple."

From this could come at least three UVP options:

1. Making your financial investing simple.
2. Clarifying complex financial decisions.
3. Simplifying your financial life.

If you're in the fresh-produce delivery business, common "why" answers in the surveys could be:

"You always get our produce there on time, every time."

"You never make a delivery mistake."

"You always care if there is a problem — which is priceless."

"You always make sure our produce is delivered while it's still fresh."

"You are careful with our cargo."

From this could emerge three possible UVP options:

1. Your fresh produce delivered fresh and on time.
2. Careful delivery of your priceless produce.
3. Problem-free delivery, fresh and on time.

Once the crafter team agrees on three or four UVP final choices, they should Google each to make they aren't trademarked or in use by anyone else in your type of business or market sector. If one is (and it hasn't happened yet), they need to change it so that yours is authentic to only your business.

You Can Vote, but Interviewed Customers Decide!

When your creative team has crafted the final three to four possible UVPs from customer input, you are ready to gather the vote. Now comes another shift in your mind-set.

Yes, the executive team gets to vote, but ultimately those best customers who were interviewed make the final selection. Here is the process to follow.

1. First, top leadership or the business owner and management meet and are briefed on the choices. A review of the process that was used helps solidify their commitment to the final UVP and its full, enterprise-wide integration.
2. The three or four final UVP candidates crafted by the team are revealed. Our experience is that this usually leads to a lively session.
3. Once the leadership reviews the crafters' choices, they have to agree that they really represent who they are and the true value of the business. Further, it is what they can and will deliver in the marketplace. A false promise is not a promise at all, it's at best a proposition.
4. The executive team will likely have one they think would be the best to use. Or they will want to offer

some edits! Of course here in the "C" suite they can have an opinion, but not a re-editing role nor the final vote. Remember, the process requires that those interviewed make the final selection via their votes.

Here's an example of getting this step right. When we helped American National discover their UVP, they had nearly one hundred surveys from their best customers. Our creative team had worked hard, crafting the final four UVP choices from their customers' "why" responses. The CEO, CMO, and other senior management met with me and my team in their boardroom for the unveiling.

They loved the choices — emotional, functional, refreshing, and clear. Each choice truly reflected who they were in the marketplace and their demonstrated values. Yet one stood out to CEO Greg Ostergren, and everyone else on his team agreed. Yes, they agreed his choice was perfect. Then he looked me straight in the eye and said: "Okay, that's what we like, but let's stay true to the process you gave us. Let's find out which one the customers we surveyed will choose. That will be our final choice."

Truly inspirational leadership skills! Decisive, empathetic, and willing to do only one thing — the right thing. I also knew at that moment he would always do the right thing to fulfill their value promise as well.

Once you have briefed senior leadership on the choices, you are ready to take them to the customers you interviewed for a vote. The UVP candidate with the most votes by your best customers wins.

Here's the right way to get the final vote right:

1. Have only those who conducted the face-to-face interviews take the choices back to those customers. Closing the loop with the same individuals who conducted the

interviews creates further customer edification as well as internal buy-in.

2. Unlike with the interview process, we have learned that announcing the choices over the phone works best. They hear it the way they expressed it.

3. Be sure to set up their vote with "Which of the statements I am about to read to you best describes what we do for you?"

4. Don't emphasize one over the other, just deliver them without demonstrating bias. After you've read them, they'll gravitate toward a clear choice.

5. Never ask for a UVP choice ranking — first, second, third, etc. — just ask for one answer. You want their choice to be clear — not sort of, kind of, or maybe! Occasionally a customer will have a word or two to offer as a substitute. Be gracious. Be keenly aware, however, that this wordsmithing may be a style, personality, or communication issue germane only to this customer. Crafted correctly, your UVP choices are a result of actual words and phrases articulated by the interviewed.

6. Compile the votes. The UVP candidate that gets the most votes from those interviewed wins. Even if only by a margin of one!

Once your best customers have made their selection and cast their vote, send each of them a heartfelt hand-written thank-you note. Accompany the note with a token gift of lasting value, such as a small quartz clock. Don't send a thank you e-mail, or flowers or wine.

Remember, a carefully handwritten thank-you note and a thoughtful gift are remembered long after an e-mail is deleted, or the wilted flowers and empty wine bottles are in the trash. Be memorable to be meaningful! These tried-and-true customers will tell their friends why they received that memorable gift from you. These same friends may even call, visit, or click to inquire about how your company delivers on your promise!

Wrap-up

With your UVP clarified and codified, you will be empowered to do mighty things within your business. It is an exciting time to be in your shoes. Now you will be inspired to break out by promoting your promise and to win the attention of potential customers and acquire their business.

However, before you begin promoting, there's still work to do to ensure you never break your unique promise of value, so keep reading!

ACTION POINTS

1. Who are your best customers?
2. Who are your most engaged customer-facing representatives?
3. If you had to name three to four creative individuals for your UVP crafting team, who immediately comes to mind?
4. Are you really ready and willing to let your best customers decide which Unique Value Promise is best for your business?

6

Step Three: Getting Your Organization on Promise

"It is an immutable law in business that words are words, explanations are explanations, promises are promises, but only performance is reality."
— HAROLD GENEEN, FORMER PRESIDENT OF ITT

THE VERY ESSENCE OF YOUR Unique Value Promise is a pledge to the customer. This commitment inspires on the one hand, but on the other, sets an expectation of outstanding performance.

This expectation is very real. Consequently, it must be met every time and at every interaction. Before you take your Unique Value Promise into the marketplace, therefore, your entire team must be on board and committed to being on promise. By doing so they'll focus on everything necessary to prove your promise is true. This in turn will firmly establish your distinct presence in the marketplace and propel you out in front of your competition.

A great example of this is Southern Air Conditioning Company, located in Florida. Their Unique Value Promise was clear — "We are on time or you don't pay a dime." Wow! A powerful promise for those who've wasted all day waiting for service people to show up — and it rhymes, too. To see how it works, I called and asked the young lady who answered the telephone how they were able to be on time. She told me that they schedule appointments far enough apart to provide a buffer for travel and unexpected or long repairs. They also have "floaters" whose job it is to make every appointment on time in case the assigned tech is delayed.

This is an example of perfect execution because their promise is not just a slogan. It's part of their corporate culture and DNA. They are all on purpose and on promise.

A Culture of Promise

To leverage the power of your promise in the marketplace and be truly distinct, you must develop an organizational culture that is purpose-driven to deliver your promise on an absolute and consistent basis. This often requires a change in the mind-set and some behaviors of your organization's staff.

Why, you may wonder? If the UVP is based on what our best customers say they already accomplish with us, isn't it already in place? Aren't we are already delivering it?

Yes and no.

There's often a difference between the experiences of best customers and the average experience of all potential customers. Often your Unique Value Promise, when uncovered, at first reflects almost an unconscious, irregular, and inconsistent level of competency in the organization. Now that it's been crafted and articulated, however, your value promise requires consistent behaviors and delivery every time! By everyone, for everyone!

This consistent and absolute culture of promise has many components, both tangible and intangible. However, just as your promise is the cornerstone and foundation of your distinct presence, a promise-centric culture is one of the key building blocks of a breakout business.

When your organizational culture is aligned with your promise, it makes your promise a reality. It determines how you run your business and its deliverables. It mandates the support that you give to customers and your team. Further, a promise-centric culture drives marketplace recognition. It delivers referrals, warm introductions, and positive word of mouth.

Ultimately you move many of your competitors' customers to you.

Culture Is Developed, Not Installed

A promise-driven culture is not something you simply install. It must be seeded, nurtured, and developed.

Every business has an existing culture of some kind. The challenge is changing or improving the culture of your current business or organization so that it can deliver your newfound Unique Value Promise. As with so many aspects of your organization's personality, emotional climate, and traditional customs, your culture starts at the top. Each unit and department in your organizational chart, large or small, is a pyramid with someone in the leadership role. So no matter what your leadership title may be—chairman of the board, CEO, CMO, COO, CAO, CFO, president, founder, or head of a department—it begins with you!

It's crucial, therefore, that within your special sphere of responsibility and influence, you paint the vision and explain the organizational benefits of your promise. You alone provide the ongoing inspiration and empowerment to integrate your Unique Value Promise into every facet of the enterprise. Make no mistake, as a leader you set the tone and reset the priorities.

Developing a Promise-Driven Team

To develop a promise-driven culture, the first step is to get your entire team informed, up to speed, and on board as soon as your customer-centric Unique Value Promise is chosen. Whether you are a Fortune 50 company, or just you and your spouse, everyone needs to know and understand how you uncovered your promise and what it means for their future.

Your culture of promise will be evolving constantly. Developing a promise-driven team is an ongoing process. This strategic approach and tactical commitment to communicate your promise throughout every facet of your company has a profound effect on your people and their understanding of the importance of consistent enterprise-wide delivery. If you have or hire people in the future who are not able to execute your promise, you risk nonperformance. But most people will change when the behavior desired is communicated effectively, taught continually, executed consistently, and compensated appropriately.

The Ritz-Carlton Hotels are a model in this area. Every employee knows and is constantly reminded of what the company's promise is and that they must always deliver it. They are educated throughout their career on how to deliver it flawlessly, and not with just one lesson, but continually. Delivering their value promise is integrated into every training component. So they really see themselves, as their motto makes clear, as "ladies and gentlemen serving ladies and gentlemen." The result is that their culture and promise exemplifies a refined experience.

Hotel service is an intense series of minute-by-minute encounters between staff and guests. In order to ensure that their Unique Value Promise is delivered quickly, the Ritz-Carlton organization has come up with a remarkable policy that permits employees to solve problems with guests on the spot. They are allowed to spend up to a set dollar amount, without anyone's approval, to take care of guest emergencies. I experienced this firsthand at the Ritz-Carlton on Amelia Island. I was there to speak at a conference, and I thought the meeting planner had arranged for a car service to take me back to the airport for a must-make flight to my next engagement. Unfortunately, at the appointed hour, the car service inexplicably was nowhere to be found, nor did they answer the phone.

The bellman then said, "Sir, we don't want you to miss your flight — I can have a cab here in five minutes." He did.

When I got to the airport, the cab driver refused payment. He said, "Oh no, the bellman at the Ritz took care of it! Seventy-five dollars worth."

Our organization has adopted this same strategic model.

Recently, members of my team were conducting a Unique Value Promise alignment three-day retreat for a new client. An hour before we were scheduled to begin, the projector the client provided failed to work. A member of my team immediately rented one from the hotel for $300 per day and charged it to our account. The head of office administration for the new client was incredulous.

"Can you just spend three hundred dollars a day without at least getting it approved?"

"Yes and no" was the reply.

"Yes, I can, and no, I don't need to ask. We all have the authority and, more importantly, the responsibility to deliver on our promise. We can't elevate your business performance if we don't have the ability and authority to elevate ours!"

When Someone Steps Away from Your Promise

To develop and deliver a culture of promise, it's essential you take nothing for granted. Individuals who appear out of step with your promise must be assessed and brought on board or managed out.

There are three typical behaviors demonstrated by those who are out of step and struggling with the changes needed with a new UVP:

1. *Confusion.* Some well-intentioned members of your staff may have trouble understanding how to behave

in this new culture of promise. They're not clear about what you want them to deliver, or why. These may be individuals who have no customer contact or who already believe they're delivering on their version of your value promise. This is usually a communication issue. To solve this problem, you must communicate specifically what you want, and make it clear why it's vital to business success! This emphatic communication helps them, first, to understand and second, to accept the education provided to deliver on your promise to customers.

2. *Frustration.* Those who don't know exactly how to deliver on your promise will struggle with the process of consistency. They may be new hires or old hands in your now "new" business. Recognize this as a skill-set issue. To solve it you must create step-by-step educational processes, the focus of which should not be just on what to do, but rather on how they can perform their part in delivering the entire organizational promise in their specific role. Various educational modalities from "work" shops to role-plays should be used to ensure understanding and execution. In addition, accountability procedures must be in place to ensure compliance.

3. *Resistance.* This third behavior is likely to come from those individuals who, no matter the level of communication and education you provide, will still push back against change. From our work in cultural integration of a value promise, it's clear that ultimately this is a motivation issue. They often do understand what you want and know how to deliver it, but for a variety of reasons, they see no personal benefit to themselves in changing the way they're doing things now. To clarify the reasons for

their lack of acceptance and to encourage buy-in, meet with them one-on-one, and consider the following:

- Explore their reasons for resisting this change. Keep in mind that any focus on past mistakes or just telling them that they're wrong won't be well received or accomplish anything. Instead, encourage them to explain their view of your UVP. Then ask them why they think they're right to continue doing things the way they always have and why they seem to resist changing. Listen for defensiveness versus openness in their response to see if they are being honest with themselves and with you.

- Ask them what they see as their career and personal goals. Be sure to write them down as a way of demonstrating your interest in what they say. Demonstrate your curiosity by asking how they see themselves achieving their goals. Listen carefully. These individuals may not be team players. If their way to accomplish their goals is all about doing things their way, make your expectations very clear.

- Then re-explain how delivering on your value promise every day will help them achieve what they want professionally and personally. You can begin with questions like, "What are three things we can do to help you execute our promise in your day-to-day activities?"

- If they still want to keep doing what they've always done, point out that not performing on your promise is not an option! Explain that allowing them to continue as they have jeopardizes your organization's distinctive place in the marketplace regardless of their role in your business.

Managing Out the Noncompliant

The vast majority of people want to do their very best, not just what is acceptable to keep their job. The introduction of your UVP will have an incredibly positive effect on human behavior. Most of your people will be inspired to perform with this newfound sense of purpose. They also will quickly realize that your value promise is in many ways a reflection of *their own* values. If you communicate achievable expectations, develop their skills, empower them to execute, and provide appropriate rewards, you will develop a promise-driven team.

On the other hand, if after putting these components in place you still have culture-resistant members on your team, you must have the courage to change personnel.

This doesn't mean moving the noncompliant individual out to the back office or a secondary location. No. It's out the door!

"Yes, but . . ." is often expressed at the point where entrepreneurs to CEOs are faced with moving one or several people out the door. They may complain that these people are "pretty good at what they do." This may be true. But if you focus on your value promise and how you intend to deliver it consistently to break out in a competitive marketplace, you'll realize these people will in fact hold you back. Remember, they have elected not to conform to the cultural changes that are in the company's best interest.

"But what about termination benefit contracts and unemployment insurance?" We've heard it all. The larger point is this: there is a greater cost if you keep the noncompliant.

I was the head of sales and marketing for *The Robb Report*, a magazine for the affluent lifestyle, in its formative years. I led fifteen individuals whose sole job was to call affluent and wealthy individuals on the telephone to help them sell their exotic cars, real estate, planes, trains (yes, we even sold a train!) by providing access to our readers through an ad in our publication. Our culture was one of respect and creative approaches. It was reflective of our promise to sellers that we would creatively "help them reach several thousand highly qualified buyers."

I had an excellent team of sales reps. However, there was one individual on my staff who was known as, and truly was, "the closer." He led the sales board every month. But as his success increased, so too did his lack of support for our culture and promise. Instead, he believed he could do things his way — tepid discovery, an aggressive, caustic, even intimidating sales approach, little ad creativity, and plenty of over-promising. Regrettably, I let him do his thing because I rationalized that I couldn't let him go and that I needed his sales volume. I gave him all the room in the world and he was our sales leader.

Then several customers complained about his disrespectful attitude, over-promising, and lack of a creative approach to help them reach buyers. But I justified it. We were the new kids on the block and we needed his ad sales revenue. But I noticed over a period of several months that not only did the customer complaints continue, but the rest of the sales force were also becoming more like him — increasingly caustic, abrasive, and over-promising on their outbound calls.

Then it hit me — I wasn't being true to our promise or to what people wanted or expected from us. We were neither respectful nor creative.

I called the "closer" into my office and asked him how I could help him refocus and execute on our promise.

"There's no reason to do anything like that," he responded. "My approach works. Tough is good."

I told him I'd made a mistake in allowing this to go on, and explained he needed to get back on our track so he could be true to our approach. I explained again what our customers expected from us. I made it clear I would support him in every way possible, but could no longer support his out-of-step approach just to drive revenue. His reply was antagonistic.

"You can't fire me, you need my sales."

Yes, he was right, I thought to myself. I do need his sales. But there'd be a greater cost if I didn't fire him. We'd lose business, and our good reputation, over time. Eventually, no one would take our sales calls or advertise with us.

Then and there I gave him every chance to accept my request and change, but ultimately he wanted to keep doing things his way. So I fired him on the spot and walked him out the door.

The result? Sales nearly doubled the next month. The other fourteen representatives realized we were truly committed to what our customers expected from us. I wasn't just giving lip service to our promise, but showed them I was committed to it!

The message here is clear: if you hire or keep people who can't or won't deliver on the expectations your UVP sets, you'll eventually fall short on your promise and never break away from your competition. So have courage, not doubt—your very future depends on it.

Make a decision and give those who are noncompliant the opportunity to work somewhere else. You might suggest they go to work for those who still think they are your competition.

Having Fun Reinforces Cultural Fundamentals

It's not just your people that contribute to your culture of promise. Another cultural component that enables the organization to deliver is the work environment. Does it facilitate esprit de corps? Is it conducive to everyone working efficiently and effectively as a team on the customers' behalf?

Also, in light of increased productivity requirements in today's workforce, is it fun to work at your business? In our firm, whoever is in "residence" at our main office in Florida has an office lunch together once a week—executives, managers, support staff—and it's all fun and no business. They order what they want and the firm picks up the tab. In addition, every quarter our entire team gathers for a daylong planning session at my Florida home near our headquarters. I articulate the strategic objectives and supportive initiatives I want to accomplish over the next ninety days. There's usually commentary from the team, particularly around expansion or contraction of the initiatives needed to accomplish the objectives. After this, the entire team works together to build out their respective departmental ninety-day tactical plans to accomplish those initiatives.

Before we start, I always cook breakfast for everyone. Lots of bacon, eggs, biscuits, and camaraderie! How about your team? All work and no fun? How is that working for you?

Cultural Alignment Creates a Purposeful Team

There are many other cultural components that enable your organization to live out its promise every day. Every detail counts: the appearance of your office, store, plant, or even the way your employees dress has a positive or negative effect on culture compliance.

Having a clear set of ethical principles by which you and your team consistently operate is a key component as well — principles that reflect your business values and value promise, even if it means turning down business. Is your team empowered to make real decisions or are they bound by a nebulous "That is our policy"? Aligning every function and action of your business so that it is solely focused on the customers' perspective is the only way to live out your promise truly and be seen as distinct from all others in the marketplace.

Magic happens when your Unique Value Promise is culturally aligned at every customer touch point. Team members constantly and proactively find many, many creative ways to reinforce the promise and resultant culture.

Two illustrations of this come to mind: Coca-Cola and Chick-fil-A.

Coke is, of course, a multinational corporation. Chick-fil-A is a midsize quick-service food business with a national footprint. If you haven't experienced their commitment to a healthy and succulent chicken sandwich, it's something to put on your bucket list! Employees of both Coca-Cola and Chick-fil-A continually demonstrate their promise-centered culture by personalizing and humanizing customer interactions.

For many years now, usually in the winter months of December, January, and February, Coca-Cola has run a series of ads featuring polar bears sliding down snow-covered hills or lounging on ice floes, drinking various Coke products. Remarkable? Not really. Funny as they burp or toss bottles of Coke? Yes! However, after these ads run, Coke gets thousands of letters from children writing to the bears. How does their team respond in a personalized and humanized way? The bears write back to every child. They also put in a coupon for Mom and Dad so they can "refresh their world."

Recently, they took their personalization and very human approach to a whole new level. Each can and bottle of Coke with special markings sold during those winter months carries a code that lets people text a one-dollar donation to the World Wildlife Fund's effort to protect the polar bears' Arctic home. Coke will match these donations up to $1 million.

Chick-fil-A follows a similar path, even though their annual sales are only slightly more than one month's worth of Coca Cola's. For years their advertising campaigns have featured funny renegade cows pleading with people to "eat mor chikin." It's engaging, cute, and a counterintuitive UVP campaign — eat chicken so you can save cows!

The result?

You guessed it. The cows get mountains of mail and yes, those cows take great pride in their ability to write back personally. They always include a coupon to be sure the child who wrote can take his or her family out to "eat mor chikin"! After all, the cows want to keep writing back!

The net result? They've had forty-three years of consecutive, positive sales growth. They also go to the next step and personalize their influence on their team members' experience as well. Every store is closed on Sunday! To honor God and support their team members' families. This demonstrates purposeful execution and promise-centric culture.

Create Promise Integration Teams

As these examples illustrate, by communicating, educating, empowering, and rewarding the integration of your UVP you will move your team to action. Nevertheless, to simply ask for or demand integration in no way accomplishes it.

That's why I recommend creating small, functional teams within your organization. Make it their job to determine how they can deliver your Unique Value Promise tangibly and intangibly at every point of customer interaction in their functional area. They will likely identify large and small changes in many areas such as marketing, sales, service, manufacturing, delivery, billing, facilities, and communications. Let them be the author of those processes. They'll tender new ideas, new procedures, and new ways to revamp processes to ensure they're more promise-centric. Be sure you give them the freedom to take action.

People support what they help build.

A Checklist to Assess Your Current Culture

To start you on the journey of performing on your promise every day, begin by assessing your existing culture. It's essential you stop, look, listen, and assess before you roll your UVP into the marketplace. A yes or a no is the only answer for each of these.

- Are you driven to deliver value from the customer's perspective more than to achieve sales results?
- Are appreciation and empathy for prospects, customers and staff evident in every single interaction?
- Are there clear communication protocols in place for feedback and team-member ownership of a customer's problems?
- Are you constantly communicating, educating, empowering, and rewarding promise-driven behaviors?
- Is your organization structured to deliver all commitments, products, and services from your buyers' perspective?
- Is your environment fun, friendly, flexible, and positive?
- Is attention to aesthetics, such as physical space and team-member attire, a part of your process to deliver your promise?

By making an honest assessment now, as you begin to implement your UVP, you'll identify issues to address and problems to solve as your culture of promise begins to grow. You'll also see specific areas and people that need to be changed.

Wrap-up

For marketplace distinction, your Unique Value Promise must be fully integrated into all facets of your organization. Yes, some changes will be needed to ensure you culturally deliver on your promise every time.

As you continue to read and study this book, you'll continue to discover how to live out your promise every day and ensure you are meeting the expectations your UVP sets in place. You'll develop a promise-centric culture that has your entire team working on purpose versus working from pressure! It will make your business distinct and create a value that is beyond calculation.

ACTION POINTS

1. Are you committed to delivering your promise every time and reinforcing it consistently through your culture?

2. Are you determined to develop a customer-centric approach in every facet of your business?

3. Is every interaction in your organization personalized and humanized in every way possible?

4. How will you address the issues that need attention based on the checklist above?

5. How will you a) communicate, b) educate, c) empower, d) compensate your team so they can live out your Unique Value Promise every day and truly ensure a distinct marketplace presence, one that compels people to inquire and buy repeatedly from you?

7

Step Four: Marketing Your Distinction

"Winning the buyer's attention is good, but getting them to inquire is pure gold!"
— MUSED ON A PARK BENCH

NOW THAT YOU HAVE CRAFTED your Unique Value Promise and forged your entire organization into a culture that can deliver that promise every time, the next step is to market and promote it to your current, lapsed, and potential new customers. The first principle I'd like you to consider in this process is using curiosity over persuasion to break out in a competitive marketplace.

Curiosity, Not Persuasion

Yes. Put aside the old conventional ideas that marketing is arm-twisting, cajoling, inveigling, or arguing your customer into making what you think is the right choice for them. No, no, no.

From this point forward you will be using your UVP to stimulate curiosity and create a compelling interest about what they can expect from your organization and its products and services. The drill is to make folks wonder: What is this company about? Who are they? How can they do this?

Consequently, how you execute and deliver on your UVP is critical. Your promotion must be varied and on purpose to be sure your target consumer is fully aware of your promise to them. Once they inquire, your sales process must be congruent with helping people get what they want. Old-school approaches and sales presentations must be modified to include deep discovery and the articulation of clear, distinct advantages and personalized benefits prospective buyers will receive from your products and services. Further, ongoing customer interactions and service responses must be elevated to solidify your distinct presence in the marketplace.

In this chapter, you'll find the building blocks needed to elevate your entire promotion platform so you can create that curiosity, that excitement about who you are and what you do in a manner that is true to your promise and creates delighted advocates.

The Importance of Well-Planned Promotion

Winning people's attention and carving out your distinct position in this noisy, ever-changing, and competitive marketplace requires single-minded dedication. With so many businesses attempting to capture customers you should have, you can't just sit and wait for people to beat a path to your door, even with a brilliant UVP.

Buyers can't inquire if they don't know you exist. You must promote constantly to make your position known and to own it outright. You have a clear responsibility to occupy the distinct position your value promise has created for your business. Your objective should be to make your business first and foremost in the potential buyer's mind. By doing so, when the window of opportunity to purchase opens, you are the first and likely the only place they will inquire.

Consequently, with your Unique Value Promise in place, promotion then serves the purpose of making the right people—the target consumer—aware of who you are and what you can achieve for them. They may be in geographic proximity to your store or office, or within an industry or demographic group you are targeting, or in a burgeoning population of people who buy online: they may be among millions of potential customers on the Web.

With the solid positioning and distinct presence of your Unique Value Promise, you enable many, many consumers to know and understand what you can and will do for them. You're no longer using old-school selling propositions. Instead, you are using your Unique Value Promise to stimulate their curiosity to inquire and begin a sales conversation.

To execute any promotion brilliantly requires forethought and good planning. Promotion without a plan is an expense without a purpose. Millions of dollars every year are wasted by organizations on promotion that is poorly thought out and doesn't work.

As my good friend, Dr. Nido Qubein, president of High Point University in North Carolina, said so well:

> Some people think success comes effortlessly, with no need for effort or conscious planning. All you need to do is be in the right place at the right time, and at some happy moment, success will fall into your lap. Such people are called failures.
>
> Successful people know that in business or any other undertaking, you must plan for success, and you must make conscious choices centered on your core values. On rare occasions, somebody also wins the multimillion-dollar lottery. But most people don't. The sure route to success lies through careful planning in harmony with a core motivation.

This reinforces the need for a comprehensive marketing and promotional plan for you and your business—a specific plan for how you are going to make your value promise known to the marketplace during the next year and every year thereafter. Then, to be sure your promotional plan is effective and executed brilliantly, you must develop a tactical plan of specific steps to be taken every ninety days to promote and deliver your promise to the market. Create one for the first ninety days of the year, the following ninety, and every ninety-day cycle thereafter to support your annual marketing plans.

Why Ninety-Day Plans?

We run our consulting, coaching, speaking, educational tools, and online learning businesses on an annual plan, but we divide it into ninety-day planning cycles. In addition, we require each of our clients to conform to the same schedule during our work with them, because that's about how far out most people can see. Certainly sixty days out is very clear. Sixty days allows for tactical steps to be detailed and assigned to accomplish each strategic objective. It gives everyone a sense of accomplishment as they check things off and move ahead.

Our clients have found this process incredibly useful and retain it after our initial project work with them ends. It gives them a clear track to follow and creates a sense of real fulfillment. From a leadership perspective, it also gives them unintended insight.

As Augie Cenname, CEO of the Cenname Team, private wealth advisers at Merrill Lynch (a Bank of America Company), said, "Richard, it helps us get things done more efficiently. But it also lets me know quickly what is not working. We adjust and continue to move forward. That in and of itself is an actionable advantage!"

Another benefit of ninety-day plans: they allow you to be far more nimble to seize on unexpected market opportunities that often arise during the course of executing your annual or floating twelve-month promotional plan. Committing to having a clear strategy for all facets of your business marketing plan backed by specific and tactical ninety-day plans and not just an ad-hoc approach is essential for real business success. To utilize ninety-day plans for the promotion of your distinctive position and other business functions, go to Readers and Resources on my website and download our ninety-day plan template. It's free and will give you the tool you need to execute this planning cycle strategy in your business.

Integrating Your Promise into Your Marketing

I'm often asked, "What is the single best way to promote a business or nonprofit to target consumers?"

My answer is: In reality, there is no singular way at all because different things and media motivate different people. What really works in today's marketplace is using a variety of media and methods with a singular message highlighting your value promise to create curiosity and interest. Also, lest you fear people will grow weary of your promise and its promotion, fear not! Remember that consumers have something to accomplish every day, and your new value promise speaks profoundly to that something for many of them.

Effective promotion requires that you and everyone in your organization write and speak in the voice, and to the emotions of, the prospect or customer. To accomplish this successfully, you must communicate with them, not talk at them. And not in generic terms but, to the extent possible, in a personalized and humanized way to encourage consumer curiosity and responsiveness.

Personalizing Your Unique Value Promise

Recognizing that the mass market has been replaced by a mosaic of niches, your UVP can be customized according to the market segment you're targeting. Here are some examples.

By Marketplace or Niche
If you are in the roofing business in several niches and your UVP crafted by interviewing your current customers is "Helping you

protect the value of your real estate investment," imagine modifying it to read "Helping homeowners protect the value of their real estate investment."

Instant positioning and curiosity!

By Specific Location

If you have a home nursing service in several geographic locations and your value promise is "Assisting individuals so they can live at home longer," you could modify it to fit each location — for example, "Assisting individuals in Falls City, Nebraska, so they can live at home longer."

By Market Sector

If you're in the security business and position your firm in the marketplace with, "Helping you keep your family safe," you can modify it to fit another market sector with "Helping you keep your law office safe."

Or if you own a midsize computer services company and your promise is "Elevating your technology platform for greater efficiency," you could modify it to specific market sectors, for example, "Elevating your technology platform for greater manufacturing efficiency" (or "food service efficiency," etc.).

For Specific Types of People or Age Groups

A holistic doctor might say, "Helping you live the life you imagine." It could be modified and personalized as "Helping senior citizens live the life you imagine."

A firm selling dental whitener and specializing in "Making your smile sparkle" could modify and personalize that UVP to read, "Making your child's smile sparkle." These kinds of modifications speak directly in the voice of the target consumer!

The key is to stay true to your authentic promise if you modify your promotion to be even more effective in a specific niche. Your modifications simply serve to give your message an even deeper resonance by personalizing it to specific markets.

Listening Constantly

Effective promotion and reinforcement of your distinct presence requires listening proactively to your buyers and prospects, not just during the UVP discovery process, but all the time.

By keeping your ear to the ground, you'll capture functional and emotional clues about your products or services that resonate and motivate buyers. Listen by every means possible, including blogs, comment cards, and debriefing customer-facing sales and service personnel. Keep improving your understanding of why consumers buy a particular product or service on a consistent basis.

An excellent approach to this with your sales and service team is not to just ask, "What did the prospect/customer say?" but rather, "Why did they say or do what they said or did?"

This trains your customer-facing team to always ask why! This is important because they'll discover the persuasive language customers use to describe why they bought a particular product or service. Customers will often articulate the specific functional advantages and emotional benefits they've gained! When incorporated into your "what" and "how" sales processes and collaterals, this kind of listening will ensure you are constantly on point.

Communicating with Clarity and Power

Effective promotion is also communicating persuasively. Customers and prospects want to understand. To ensure you communicate clearly, persuasively, and with power, use vibrant words and phrases in your copy. This helps customers see the relevance of your products and services clearly. Lively verbs like these bring energy and persuasiveness to any copy or text:

Prepare	Structure	Select	Set
Increase	Foster	Make	Change
Identify	Build	Master	Improve
Define	Conduct	Write	Monitor
Create	Play	Overcome	Transfer
Interface	Demonstrate	Handle	Get
Develop	Explore	See	Find
Last	Draft	View	Sketch
Distinguish	Use	Pinpoint	Apply
Perform	Describe	Focus	Organize
Match	Determine	Divide	Examine
Design	Train	Avoid	Start-up

In addition, many of your marketing collateral pieces will serve the purpose of explaining how you deliver on your Unique Value Promise. In the past, this usually meant listing your business attributes and product or service features. But today don't just list them. Be sure to include the specific persuasive advantages and benefits each delivers to your target consumers.

A perfect bridge phrase is "And what this means to you is . . . !"

For example, if you are in the real estate business and your discovered UVP is "Making your dream home a reality," you'll want to write about what that means and how you accomplish that in your explanatory marketing collateral.

What you might normally write regarding how you deliver your promise is, "We search the entire Multiple Listing Service for you." Good. But you can write even more persuasively and with additional clarity. How about "We search the best choices so you can make the right choice." Now they not only know what you do for them and how you do it, but you are verifying that you can make their dream home a reality, functionally and emotionally. You are communicating that your value promise is achievable. They see the value of your attributes and features. They see that you can deliver what they want.

Of course, not all marketing collateral pieces are appropriate for explaining how you deliver on your promise. But whenever it is appropriate, close the loop! Leave nothing to chance. It inspires consumers to respond, to inquire and start a purchase discussion.

The list of ways to promote your UVP is limited only by your imagination. However, the better you know and understand how to reach your target consumer, the more creative and effective your promotion will be. Use every means available to deepen your understanding of how best to communicate with them. What media do they interface with on a regular basis? How do they like to receive messages, and which methods deliver the best reach and response? You can gather this data online as well as glean it from your UVP survey questions or other customer interfaces.

There are also numerous sources readily available from industry associations and special-interest groups that support your target consumer — be sure to utilize them.

Armed with good research on your intended customers, and your distinctive UVP in your hip pocket, your creative juices will be in overdrive as your ideas expand and flourish. However, stay committed to integrating your value promise into everything you do. Also, keep in mind that integrating your UVP into all your marketing efforts takes time. That's why the ninety-day planning process mentioned earlier is so effective.

Little Things That Make a Big Difference

You'll never feel overwhelmed if you achieve a full integration on an incremental basis. Remember the marathoner's creed? "Inch by inch, anything is a cinch; yard by yard, it's miles too hard." That said, here are crucial ways to travel your promotional path on a moment-by-moment basis.

E-mail

Every member of your staff should have your Unique Value Promise as part of their electronic signature, right below their name. You spend a fortune to place it prominently on your stationary and other correspondence pieces, right? Why omit this communication medium? Be relentless!

Every e-mail, regardless of who sends it out, reaches someone who is in some way connected to you or your organization. Leverage this golden opportunity to position your firm, reinforce your value promise, and get the word out.

Inbound Voicemail Greeting

Using your promise as part of your inbound voicemail greeting will solidify your value in the minds of those reaching out to you. Further, it reinforces verbally the idea that you are the source for what the caller hopes to accomplish. And when you articulate your value promise in your office telephone or business cell phone greeting, people will often leave you a message that explains exactly what they want and how to do business with them.

When you call our corporate office after hours, currently you'll hear: "Thank you for calling Richard Weylman's office and the Weylman Consulting Group. We look forward to elevating your business performance in today's marketplace."

As a result, many people leave messages that begin, "Thanks, that's why I am calling you. We want to elevate our performance and we need help with . . ." or "We want Richard to speak at our conference to help us understand today's marketplace."

You can inspire and encourage people by integrating your Unique Value Promise into your inbound messaging. You create instant value and generate enthusiasm: the potential customer can feel she's found the place to get the outcome she desires. Just be prepared for the long "I need you to . . ." or "I need help with . . ."

messages! Yes, they are pure gold! Their messages really set your
return calls in motion in the right way. You are fully prepared to
focus on them and deliver on your value promise.

Outbound Voicemail Messages

When you're leaving initial messages for customers or prospects,
be sure to articulate your promise.

For example: "Mrs. Wilson, we look forward to speaking with
you about our new spring line and 'helping you get the look you
want.'" In subsequent messages, when you are calling back, give
additional details and reinforce your promise: "Mrs. Wilson, our
new spring line is in and you will have" — not "we" have; remember, it is about them — "an amazing choice of colors and styles from
which to choose so we can 'help you get the look you want!' I can't
wait to see you."

This will set your message apart and distinguish it from all others. You are articulating the outcome they want from their perspective. Our experience with this type of approach to initial and
subsequent calls is that people call back much more quickly.

As motivational speaker Tony Robbins has been saying for
years, people do things for "pain or pleasure." Unfortunately most
voice messages are about "I need," "I want," and "I have," and bring
you my pain. This new approach gives them pleasure. Customers
prioritize their call-backs, just like you do. The pleasurable ones
get called first. The obtuse, second. The painful ones . . . last, if at
all.

Your Website

It is amazing how many organizations and businesses spend thousands of dollars designing websites that look good and are referred
to as user-friendly. Yet the evidence of short visits to most of these
websites is well documented. The average website home page visi-
tation, as of this writing, is less than thirty-three seconds.

Sure, some consumers click through. Others click away, having reached your site in error. But all too often qualified prospects also click away to another site. To capture click-throughs there must first be a compelling reason for them to stay and look around. Use your value promise to capture their interest and create a desire to stay. Most websites, even full-blown retail sites, have their business name on the home page and lots of text about who they are and how well they do things. Then there's a full-court press to get customers to inquire or grab a "shopping cart."

In contrast, your website home page should prominently display your Unique Value Promise. It must be one of the very first things people see when they find your home page! With your UVP clearly visible, you'll immediately capture their interest and curiosity.

But the prominent display of your UVP is only the first step for your potential customer. Think about the experience people will have on your site:

- Is it designed so that it is easy to navigate and search?
- Does it educate and motivate?
- Are you writing and speaking *to* them or *at* them?
- Are you telling them how you will deliver their desired end result in a clearly delineated way, using a combination of visual and text components?
- Are you speaking with prospective customers in their language or in industry jargon and acronyms?
- Is your site and message sticky, personalized, engaging, and clearly positioning you as distinct?
- Do you have a blog or other contact method where they can ask questions easily? (This in itself is a terrific interactive listening tool and will help you stay relevant!)
- Do you have a useful report or sampler to entice and compel visitors to engage with you and share their e-mail ad-

dress for further connection? An e-mail or opt-in opportunity to receive this document is very effective.

- Do you avoid creating a pop-up on your page to capture
their e-mail? Pop-ups often irritate viewers and they click
away. Instead, present compelling copy to motivate them
to opt-in to receive something of value such as "10 Mistakes to Avoid" or "Five Ideas to . . ." or a bimonthly tip to
achieve something.

- Can they view your site on their smartphone or mobile
device clearly and distinctly? More and more consumers want the information, the solution, and the provider's
name now, not later. Or as Howard Van Bortel, a dear late
mentor of mine, said years before the Internet came into
play, "If I wanted it tomorrow, I would order it tomorrow!" Imagine how many consumers feel this way today.

Value-Based URLs

Going a step further, some companies and organizations that "get
it" own URLs that drive consumers to them. They know that people are hunting online for answers, solutions, and promise-driven
providers. The URLs they purchase are designed to redirect those
people to them.

One of my favorites is www.GetMeJustice.com — owned by a
law firm, of course. It's pretty clear that there are plenty of people
seeking some sort of justice. With the unlimited availability and
low cost of most URLs, there are many opportunities in the virtual world. You can and should get your name and promise out
through multiple redirected URLs. Buying a URL that is laden
with promise and oriented to your business drives people to you.

Fortunes are spent on search optimization and key words. Yet
solution-oriented URLs that could redirect often sit on the side-
lines. Interestingly, www.INeedaLaugh.com is available as of this

writing—isn't that what a comedy club or comedian provides? Re-directed, wouldn't that put them squarely and distinctly in front of their target audience?

Here is one I've seen recently out of the many other URLs that drive buyers to the owning company: www.GarageDoorRepair-Guy.com.

Imagine multiple URLs that redirect buyers to your business website when they want to accomplish something. Once there, the first thing they see is your promise that speaks to exactly why they're looking in the first place.

Social Media

Facebook, YouTube, LinkedIn, and Twitter have all become vehi-cles to interact with and deliver your promise to large constituent groups. Social media is relational marketing in its purest form. But in our lightning-fast world of hand-held connectivity and commu-nication, you must keep your content updated, relevant, and fresh to make it effective as a promotional tool and to ensure you are seen as quick and relevant.

To be effective with social-media marketing, therefore, you need to interact continually. This means a "most recently updated" notice can't be a month old. The trick is to balance your workload so that you spend a limited but regular amount of time on social media on a regular basis, including:

1. Facebook

Your Facebook page should display your Unique Value Promise and encourage your customers to "like" you. Building a large base can imply value and that implication, coupled with your customer-centric UVP, is often all the proof people need to go to your web-site and order or inquire.

Also, commentary or feedback from current customers who "friend" you should speak to why they do business with you.

Google is currently ranking businesses based upon what people say about them on the social networks. There are of course other factors they use to rank businesses for search optimization. But this ranking is one you can influence, based on direct input from your customers.

Remember that customer testimonials should not be about how good you are, but rather how doing business with you is good for them. Suggesting this up front when seeking feedback works wonders. So suggest that they explain what they have accomplished through you or your business. Ask them to articulate why that's important to them, or have them tell you their story. This gentle and subtle turn of request points them in the right direction.

2. YouTube

YouTube boasts the second largest number of queries in the world, after Google. But you must be right on-point with your message. Most YouTube video clips are funny or entertaining or, at the very least, informative with an interesting delivery.

Remember to keep your YouTube video short and simple, not more than three to five minutes. Don't worry about Hollywood production standards. The millions of YouTube devotees don't care about fancy camera work or scripted voice-overs. Just be authentic, clear, and consumer-focused.

No matter which approach you use, be sure your promise is part of the message. Incorporate it at the close of the video (as in "sponsored by") or think creatively of other ways to weave it into the presentation. Millions are spent by companies to place their products in television shows and movies. Countless more invest in public and sports venue signage to get visibility.

Why not combine the two without the expense? Have your promise on signage in the background of your video. Subtle, subconscious, and effective.

Be certain that your videos aren't about how good you are.

Rather, use them to entertain, inform, or educate viewers. They'll quickly see your value — particularly if your message is engaging — and will forward your link to others. To be distinct and viral can lead to breakout explosive growth!

3. LinkedIn

LinkedIn is another tool designed to expand your network and to get your "net" working. Building a base of linked customers and prospects enables you to communicate with them in distinctive ways. As an example, you can send personalized e-mails on value-added topics that are important to them. It also expands your reach into potential new markets.

Be sure your profile isn't just about you — your title and vitae. Rather, integrate your promise into your description and vitae. Again, write *to* the reader, not *at* them. This approach ensures that you are consumer-centric, not me-centric. It also creates curiosity, interest, and numerous inquiries.

4. Twitter

Then, of course, there is Twitter! Your first reaction may be, "Who has time! It can take over your life."

But Twitter can be a powerful tool to deliver your UVP and distinct presence to vast target audiences. It's also ideal for engagement with and responsiveness from colleagues, customers, peers, and those tracking key words and responding to them.

Remember: different things motivate different people. My experience is that Gen X and Y and many, many other consumers like to follow and be in touch through this medium. We tweet regularly.

Note I said "we." Yes, I tweet, but with my extensive travel schedule I also assign a staff person to tweet messages, ideas, and thoughts that are of value to our customers and prospects. We also tweet active links about various business performance issues of interest to our followers. By so doing, we get many new followers through retweets to their fellow tweeters.

You can do this, too. You can create a daily or weekly "twitamin," which is a tweet that contains useful knowledge that is easy to take in and remember. You can provide links to useful sites to advance your position in the marketplace.

For example, if you are in the organic food business, you can tweet ideas and links about farmers, wholesalers, or helpful recipes and healthy-living sites. Or if you are in the printing business, you can tweet design ideas and links to creative-recycling paper sites. Tweeters will retweet them for you, if they see the value. This is excellent word of mouth and it does give you a distinct presence.

5. Video Business Cards

Today's consumers are very visually oriented. Recently we worked with Masterson, Emma & Associates in Naples, Florida, to help them discover their UVP and create a distinct presence in their marketplace.

Once their Unique Value Promise was solidified, they produced a unique brief video business card that clearly conveyed their promise to clients and prospects alike. It began with their UVP prominently displayed on the screen. Then they explained it was not just a slogan or tagline, but a promise to each family or individual that worked with them. They further explained that they didn't create it — their longstanding clients did. Then they showed how they deliver on their promise, from the viewers' perspective. This approach and use of media has further set them apart in the marketplace.

They've also posted their video business card on YouTube to broaden their reach and make it accessible to every prospect. Your use of a video business card should be formatted in a similar style: always speaking to the consumer's perspective.

Tracking Social Media Return on Investment

Tracking return on investment from social media can be done to some degree by using metrics of various types. Tracking opt-in e-mails and sources of new customers are just two of many. To really understand the effectiveness of social media, however, it's also essential to train your team, to ask when they interact with new customers, "How did you hear about us?"

Of course, not every benefit of social media can be quantified, but in today's mobile world, you need to be there. It is not only about what you might gain, it is also about not losing new buyers because they don't find you where they're used to looking: online. So think of social media as being as essential as your cell phone.

Go forth as a digital optimist and be there so that buyers can find your promise and your business every day.

Traditional Marketing

It's so important to stay up to date with the latest social-network innovations online. But don't forget how powerful conventional marketing can still be. Look around and listen carefully. You'll see and hear it everywhere around you. Here are some great types that are still effective.

1. Signage

Driving along the highways and byways across the globe, we're inundated with signs of every size, shape, color, and description. As in real estate, signage location, location, location is the central mantra.

Agreed. However, signage that just states your company name gives you little to no payback on the fortune you may have invested for the location. Make your signage stand out. Be sure your name and value promise are the *most* prominent images on the sign. Why? It captures the attention of those going by and prompts them to want to know more about your business. It compels a passerby's desire to check you out. This curiosity drives visits or calls to your store or business. The other most prominent item on large signage should be your telephone number (or your website).

Unfortunately, many signs go to the extreme in the other direction. They have so much detail about what you do and how you do it that in order to get it all, people would have to pull over, stop the car, and sit and read for a few minutes. Not a particularly effective approach in this busy, faster-is-better world we live in.

2. Advertising Campaigns

This is a big topic with lots of applications.

Where and when you advertise is a choice you make based on the constituents you wish to reach. No matter where you advertise — on the Web, in papers or newsletters, in trade or specialty magazines, on television, via specialized or satellite radio, or through the mail — you have to capture the attention of the people.

This is true with flyers, mailers, vehicle wraps, or any other medium. Advertising must be compelling, informative, and at the same time, worth the time it takes to read. Anything less and it won't give you the ROI or distinction you deserve.

To ensure you capture consumers' interest, your UVP should always be the headline — the thing they see first. People read, listen to, and watch ads that start with a headline. This includes both positional advertising and direct-response advertising. Each serves its own purpose (as evidenced by their descriptive names). However, the lines between them have become blurred. A positional ad that doesn't carry your value promise will in no way advance your distinctiveness in the marketplace. It may be smart, trendy, and visually appealing. But you are not in a beauty contest. You are in the "get people to know what they can really accomplish through your distinctive business and its products" contest. Same with response advertising. If you don't first capture their attention with your UVP, it's likely they won't read long enough to want to respond.

About a year ago, I met a dentist who had opened a new practice in Kahala, Oahu. He said he had spent several thousand dollars on ads in the newspaper and local lifestyle magazines announcing his new practice. When I asked him how that had worked for him, he admitted that, unfortunately, it hadn't produced many results. One look at the ads, though, said it all! A picture of a dental chair and an announcement of his new practice with a long list of what he did. And all in dental speak, I might add. The chair alone made me turn away from the ad.

This dentist would have been far better off with a headline that displayed his customer-centric value promise, if he had one then. He does now: "Make your smile as bright as a day in paradise." Today it is hard to get an appointment with him.

3. Expo and Trade Shows

The right trade shows and expos work because attendees are your exact target consumers. Exhibiting at such events, therefore, will provide you the opportunity to meet large numbers of prospects face-to-face.

The challenge, however, is that your display will be just one of many that attendees see. They glance momentarily at each booth to see why they should stop. "Why, why, why" is the silent mantra running through their minds. So many booths and tables, an avalanche, a tsunami of colorful, crowded, noisy input. It can be overwhelming and exhausting.

What they're looking for is something or someone that speaks to their perspective, someone who will help them accomplish what they are looking to do. Be it solve, identify, clarify, or experience, they are looking. Happily, many human dynamics come into play.

It starts with getting your booth placed where visitors can't miss it. Usually the right side of an aisle as they enter from the main entrance is best. Corners are terrific, too. Most importantly, be sure your Unique Value Promise is placed in the most prominent position within your display. Treat it as your headline. It's your compelling reason that will stop them in the aisle to inquire. Yes, your value promise alone will prompt them to stop. Ah, the power of curiosity!

If it's not possible to headline your promise prominently, such as across the top of your display, then adjust: stand in the aisle, as an attendee would, and face your display. Place your UVP on the left side of your display as you face into the booth. Most people read left to right. (Among the very few exceptions to this are some Orthodox Jews, the Japanese, and most Arabic people — they read right to left.) By placing it on the left, you capture their attention immediately. Then place your products, services, or attributes signage on the right (facing in). This positioning will prompt many of those drifting down the aisle to stop and inquire.

This placement of expo and trade show signage also illustrates one other important point: the need to know your audience.

Some years ago I spoke at a *Success* magazine conference for entrepreneurs. A question came up about trade-show displays, specifically sign placement. I answered the question essentially the same way I wrote it here, including the exception about reading right to left for some Orthodox Jews, the Japanese, and most Arabic people. As soon as I finished answering the question a small woman in traditional Orthodox Jewish garb stood up and said, "Thank you. We are in the jewelry business and we know the people at the shows who really understand us. They write the way we read, so we only visit those booths!"

A few more quick points about trade shows and expos to engage and improve results:

- Put away the chairs. Instead, get out to the edge of the aisle in front of your booth.

- Greet everyone who passes by! In business today, friend-raising precedes fundraising.
- Thus, your goal is to meet, greet, and gain inquiries. Put your display tables at the back of the booth, not across the front. If you don't, they act as a barrier to interaction.
- Avoid distributing brochures and flyers. Everyone knows they almost never make it out of the hall or hotel. Plus, they diminish your ability to follow through. The goal is not to pass out brochures. It's to network and communicate with prospects, capture their curiosity, discover their issues, and schedule next-step appointments! If information is needed or requested, fine. Every night, after the show, send the information to their home or office via e-mail or overnight service. It will separate you from all the others and demonstrate that you are responsive. Some research indicates trade-show requests for information can take up to eight to nine weeks to be answered.
- Contact every prospect within three to five days after the show concludes. Avoid calling to "follow up" or to see if they got the information. Instead, call them to discuss the next step needed to solve their issues and to deliver on your value promise.

4. Brochures/Catalogs/Online Stores

If your organization is creating any type of corporate brochure or product catalog, be sure to position and promote your promise here as well, to capture consumers' curiosity. This is also true of any online shopping or other product offering tools. The conventional way to create these types of marketing media has been to explain your business and its offerings in detail. To accomplish this, the design team creates a business- or offering-centric piece.

To be effective with consumers today, however, these tools should not be solely about you or your products. Think of them instead as infomercials on paper or online. They must be written from the consumer's perspective to communicate real outcomes.

To be most effective, your brochure, product catalog, or online store should start right up front with your Unique Value Promise. Consumers know what they are looking for and why they are buying. Capture their curiosity and reinforce their interest immediately. Your UVP on the front cover or on the opening online shopping page prompts buyers to continue. Curious, they then want to read and discover how you can deliver what it is they want to accomplish. On the next page tell them about your business and your qualifications. However, be careful to write your vitae from their perspective. As an example, my twenty-five years in the real estate business enables me to educate my buyers on what constitutes good value for their money.

By writing from this perspective you immediately create value. You put the focus back on them. But be brief! Less is more. Follow your vitae with the descriptions of each product or service you offer. In a product catalog or online store, as in a brochure, be sure to illustrate specific outcomes people receive from each product or service.

Be sure to write from the reader's point of view when describing each of your offerings. As an example, you may have twenty-four-hour service, and this ensures your customers always have a safety net if anything ever malfunctions with their furnace. This approach captures their interest and keeps it. Avoid long explanations. Don't get hung up on tedious details that people won't read. They may want a fine watch that keeps time accurately, but they don't want to know all the details regarding exactly how it stays accurate. The approach to take is one of describing your product or service and its ability to provide a real outcome versus explaining every nuance in deep detail.

5. Replacing Cover Letters or E-mails

I've never understood why brochures, catalogs, requests for proposals, and all manner of sales and marketing communications
are sent with a cover letter or cover e-mail. Why cover your best
work?

Cover letters and cover e-mails should be discarded and replaced with sales letters and sales e-mails! Instead of saying, "Here
is the information you requested . . ." start right off winning their
business from word one.

The first or second sentence of every sales letter or e-mail is
the attention grabber. If you can't grab potential buyers' attention by the second sentence they will either a) throw it in the
trash or b) just set it aside and never look at it again. This includes even those communications you send out in response to
an inquiry.

Consequently, every sales letter or e-mail should carry your
value promise within the first two sentences. "We look forward to
. . ." or "We are delighted to have the opportunity to . . . (your UVP
here)!" Then be pithy, to the point, and articulate next steps — less
is more!

As an aside, we never title our response to a request for proposal as a response only. Within the RFP format, we always position our response as "Our Action Plan." Why? Proposals sell, action plans solve! If you believe in your value promise, you know
you can solve. So why hope to just sell? I have never understood
why most sellers don't see themselves as solvers.

Start every RFP off with a headline — specifically your name,
followed by your UVP, as in "Submitted by Weylman Consulting
Group — Elevating Business Performance in Today's Marketplace."
If appropriate, modify your UVP to the organization or company
requesting the RFP.

Follow your headline with the words, "Our Action Plan." Then when you write, follow their RFP format, but write *to* them. Do your research on the organization requesting the proposal. Tell them what you *will* do versus what you *can* do. Point out exactly what that means to them and how they will benefit. Engage them by being positive in tone, transparent, and authentic. Take requests for proposals and turn them into requests to purchase.

6. Special Events

Every business can and should find ways to connect to the community or markets they are targeting. Becoming part of your target customer's network increases credibility and visibility.

In addition, engaging your team in proactive marketing events increases camaraderie and reinforces your customer-centric culture. It makes your team feel a part of something larger than themselves.

The sky is the limit with these occasions. You may choose to be part of a charitable or cultural event in your area. You may want to host a client-and-prospect dinner to advance your name and value to a smaller group. You can also do marketing events at your place of business. Educational events, sampling events, trunk shows, special guest speakers, monthly lunches . . . the list is endless, and so is the impact! In all cases, be sure all your PR, invitations, and collateral promotional items carry your name and UVP, but do not overshadow the event. You want your name to become synonymous with giving — not to get, but giving to have the opportunity to give again.

What Else Touches Your Customers?

There may be other, as yet unrealized ways that your UVP can reach consumers and create the curiosity to inquire. Take an objective, critical view of everything you use that touches your prospects and customers, everything from your business cards, news-

letters, stationery, thank-you notes, customer surveys, needs or
issues discovery documents, statements, applications, and shipping labels; from advertising specialty items like pens and ball caps
to vehicle and sports park signage, your company uniforms, and
water bottles.

Look at your napkins or your paper, plastic, or reusable bags.
Are you communicating your promise on each of them? Every
time? All the time?

How about your invoices? Are you talking about what *you* want
to accomplish (for example, pay their bill) or what *they* will accomplish? As an example, our invoices read, "It is a privilege helping you elevate business performance in today's marketplace! Here
is the amount due to help you to continue to move forward!" We
have found this to be far more effective than the traditional cheer-
less invoice form.

Always remember that to promote your business effectively, the
magic is in the mix. Different approaches and types of media do
motivate different people. By taking a multiple-touch-point approach, you leave nothing to chance. You never know which one
a prospective customer will see and say, "Wow, how do they do
that?" At that point, curiosity kicks in and they will inquire.

Wrap-up

There are, and will continue to be, many new ways to market your
business and get your Unique Value Promise known and visible
to consumers. Your objective must be to search constantly for
opportunities to position your business distinctly to keep it first
and foremost in the mind of the potential buyer. By continually
promoting your promise, you connect to consumers' emotional
mind-set. This will engage them deeply because you're communicating solely from their perspective. You will capture their curiosity. You'll inspire them to engage in a sales conversation with you

or your team, or to visit your website. Then, as you describe what you do and how you deliver what they want to accomplish with the products and services you offer, you'll win their business.

Read on to ensure that when those inquiries come in, your sales presentations are persuasive, value-laden, and from the buyer's perspective as well. You certainly don't want to use old-school product-centric sales presentations in today's consumer-centric world.

ACTION POINTS

1. Are you committed to solidifying your distinct presence and position, using every type of promotional tool and medium available?
2. Will your promotional messaging be written to buyers?
3. Will you communicate with clarity and power?
4. When will you review every current communication consumers see or hear to ensure it carries your UVP and positions you distinctly to break out in a competitive marketplace?

8

Step Five: Advantage-Based Selling

"The only way on earth to influence other people is to talk about what they want and show them how to get it!"
— DALE CARNEGIE

'VE SPENT MY ENTIRE ADULT life on the front lines facing the customer. And it's clear to me that no matter what you sell or to whom you sell it, you have a tremendous advantage if you know exactly why people want to buy your product or service.

If you know what your customers want to accomplish — facilitate a routine, solve a problem, clarify a chore, create an identity, experience a thrill, or any number of other things they want to do — your entire focus can shift to helping them accomplish that goal. I call this advantage-based selling.

Sales legend, the late Zig Ziglar, said it well: "Help people get what they want and you will get what you want." And Dale Carnegie said it again in a profound way in his legendary work, *How to Win Friends and Influence People:*

Thousands of salespeople are pounding the pavements today, tired, discouraged and underpaid. Why? Because they are always thinking only of what they want. They don't realize that neither you nor I want to buy anything. If we did, we would go out and buy it. But both of us are eternally interested in solving our problems. And if salespeople can show us how their services or merchandise will help us solve our problems, they won't need to sell us. We'll buy. And customers like to feel that they are buying — not being sold.

I learned the consequences of thinking only about what I wanted many years ago, when I was selling Saladmaster cookware. I loved the cookware and just knew I could sell it. I was fully committed to this new business opportunity. I saw it as my ticket from flipping burgers to having my own small business.

I worked hard and learned about the product. I even learned how to demonstrate the cookware by cooking meals in prospects' homes! But, after twelve demonstrations and twelve consecutive nos, I wondered why people weren't getting out their checkbooks and buying the cookware. I thought people weren't buying from me because they didn't understand the product. What was wrong with them?

After much thought, I realized that nothing was wrong with them. They understood what Saladmaster cookware was and how it worked. The challenge was me. I wasn't discovering why they were interested in a new set of cookware. Worse yet, I wasn't articulating, in *their* words, the functional advantages and emotional benefits of this great cookware. I wasn't clarifying or communicating what they would actually accomplish by having a set in their home. I was focused on what I wanted — making the sale — not on understanding why they wanted to buy.

When I had this revelation about advantage-based selling, I began to ask customers what they really wanted in a set of cookware. As a result, I stopped talking about the cookware or the meal I'd cooked. I stopped trying to convince them to buy Saladmaster because it was waterless cooking. I didn't talk incessantly about the beauty or construction of the pots, or say that if they damaged one there was a lifetime guarantee.

Instead, I answered their questions and explained the many advantages and benefits of Saladmaster pots—from their point of view. I discovered that good taste and good health were their biggest concerns. People began calling me to inquire how they could find out more about "cooking healthier tasty meals for their families." As a result, they bought nearly every time. They didn't buy the cookware, they bought the advantages and promised results! Most importantly, they told their friends, family, and colleagues. No one called for a set of cookware or to help me out by buying a set. No, they called for the outcome they wanted. I learned that a product-feature approach and a get-what-I-want mind-set leads to buyer indecision or a no.

Finding Out What People Really Want

Your compelling value promise prequalifies customers. People make that first visit, they pick up the phone and call or otherwise inquire because of what they've heard or read about your unique promise of value to them. By doing so they demonstrate a level of interest in your products or services.

This first contact is only the beginning of the sales conversation, however. To ensure a successful conclusion, you must probe deeply to uncover the real deep-seated reason why they inquired and what they really want to accomplish. This gives you the advantage to close the sale, to show these curious and interested consumers why they should make the purchase.

Successful breakaway businesses and their salespeople today constantly probe buyers and assess what they want and why. These businesses grow because they learn what people really want to accomplish at a deep level, and then respond quickly to deliver it.

A friend of mine in Hawaii recently bought a healthy-snack gift basket for her boyfriend's birthday. There are several places to purchase ready-made baskets where she lives. I asked her why she bought it at the With Our Aloha gift shop in Honolulu. Her reply was revealing.

She explained that she heard the shop lets the customer hand-pick items to personalize their basket. It was important to her that she only got things her boyfriend would appreciate and enjoy. I then asked how it went. She said:

> Not only did they let me do that, they asked me whom I was giving the basket to and why. I told them, and they then asked me if I had a theme or message in mind. I told them I wanted him to have many more birthdays, so I wanted only healthy snacks. Then they handed me a list of healthy items to help guide me. They asked me if I had found everything I needed. When I said "Yes, everything and more," they offered to gift-wrap it.

She added that she would tell everyone she knew about this place. Their probing helped her accomplish her goal, which in turn, of course, helped them accomplish theirs.

As a sales, marketing, or service rep, discovering what buyers want to accomplish and why it is important to them connects directly to their psychological need for meaning and significance. When approached in this manner, potential customers recognize that you want to know and understand them. They feel functionally connected and emotionally secure. They sense that you care about them. This tells them that you are going to help them accomplish what they need and want to get done.

This approach builds great relationships, repeat customers, and ultimately legendary distinctive businesses. Further, with deep discovery of what they want to accomplish and why, buyers focus more on the advantages and benefits your products or services deliver and less on the price or fee.

Using Trilogy Questions for Deeper Discovery

Today, it takes a new approach to discover a customer's real reason for considering a purchase of your products or services. It's not enough to ask one question such as "What is the one thing you want to accomplish by rewiring your garage?" or "Why are you thinking about remodeling your home?" These types of questions don't deliver the functional and emotional insight you need.

The best approach to broad-based questioning is to use trilogy-style questions. Trilogy-style questioning means your opening question begins with, "What are three things you want, need, desire, hope to accomplish," and the like. Some examples are, "What are three things most important to you when you upgrade your computer systems?" "What are three things you are looking for in a new car?" "What three things do you want addressed in your estate plan?"

By using trilogy-style questioning you expand the discovery process. When you use trilogy questions correctly, potential buyers typically will explain in great detail why they want to buy your product or service. Consequently, you will know exactly how to guide them to a purchase.

Trilogy-style questions can take on many different forms. They can even be disruptive, as in, "What are three things you wish were different with your current CPA," or "What are three things you would like to have us do that your previous property manager was not doing?"

You can also integrate your UVP when you probe customers. For example, "What are three things you are concerned about now that seem to prevent you from elevating business performance in today's marketplace?" or "What are three things you want in your dream home?"

Even if people walk in your door or call on the phone and ask you in conversation how you deliver your value promise you can simply say, "To make sure I answer your question correctly, what are three reasons why (repeat your UVP) is important to you?"

Regardless of form, trilogy questions deliver consistent results. They provide you the advantage of seeing things clearly from your potential customers' perspective, which in the end is critical to guiding them successfully to a purchase.

Trilogy questions support advantage-based selling by giving you:

- A broader and yet deeper discussion and discovery.
- A full exposition of the reason(s) the prospect is considering doing business with you.
- Increased understanding about what they really want to accomplish.
- Clarity about how you can help them get what they want.
- Momentum to move inquiries to purchase decisions.

From our longtime experience utilizing trilogy questions, as well as receiving extensive feedback from the thousands of sales professionals we have educated, several things have become clear:

1. When prospects are asked what three things are important to them, the first two answers are usually generic, off-the-cuff, obtuse values and preferences, not always meaningful in the final decision — good service, experience, and so on.

2. After their two initial answers, they may say they can't think of anything more.

At this point you are facing a psychological stall. Customers usually *do* have a third answer, and it's probably the one most important to them, the one that, if you uncover and address it, will close the purchase. Yet they're very often reluctant to reveal it. Yes, they just need time to think. But primarily, it's really a residual skepticism, even with a clear UVP, that you or your business can actually address what they really want to accomplish with a purchase. They may also feel vulnerable and cautious about giving you this essentially personal reason why they want to buy when it's this early in your relationship.

3. To overcome this stall, give them some psychological relief. After the first two answers, change the subject: "Okay, and by the way, how did you hear about us?" Or: "How long have you lived in the area?" Or any other off-topic question that will shift the conversation to neutral ground. After they answer that question and you have a short conversation around it, then simply ask, "By the way, what was the third thing you were interested in solving (creating, experiencing, etc.)?" or "What else is important to you besides the things you mentioned?" Having received some psychological relief, people will often provide you with the answer you need. Listen carefully to that final answer, though. It's usually the deeply rooted functional and emotional reason why they inquired. It nearly always aligns to your promise. Answer this and you will have both a new customer and a fan.

To be effective with this technique, it's essential that you create and then practice trilogy questions germane to your business. When I was the head of sales and marketing for the *Robb Report* in its early days, one of my sales reps who happened to be a recreational pilot gave me a great way to remember what to do when prospective customers stall with their third answer. He said to envision you're flying a plane that goes into a stall. The solution is to drop your nose and only then add power — a fitting analogy. However you remember this deep-probe technique, be sure to use it every time.

Remember also the example in which I sold a Rolls-Royce to the celebrity who wanted it boxed and wrapped for his wife's birthday . . .

Moving from Discovery to Closure

For years, well-articulated and well-used features and attendant generic benefits of products and services were usually enough to move consumers to a purchase decision. Not any longer! Sales presentations today must be fully aligned to not only support your UVP but to fully clarify that you have what buyers want.

Consequently, in this new "the consumer rules" era, sales presentations and mind-sets must shift fully to your customers' perspective. In every presentation (or, as I prefer to call them, purchase conversation) only one perspective matters—theirs. Not yours, not the company's, only the customer's perspective. After deep discovery with trilogy questions, you have the information you need to turn a prospect into a purchaser.

A sales rep for a client of ours, Insul-Sales of Ontario, illuminated how to communicate value solely from the buyer's perspective some years ago. I had the privilege of consulting with them in their roofing and insulation division. They had a superstar, a legendary roofing pro, a man named Lorrie, who was revered for his ability to sell to just about everybody. Legend had it customers acted like it was free when he sold them a new roof. They raved about the new roof even before it was installed.

I was determined to discover how Lorrie outperformed his peers. Did he have a technique or method that could be duplicated or was his a unique personality? So, when we met, I asked him about his incredible success and closing ratio.

"Look at this," Lorrie replied, pointing to an empty box of Fab laundry detergent on his desk. I didn't understand.

"What does that mean?"

"It keeps me focused on why people buy from me!"

Still confused, I asked, "How does it do that?"

"Everybody else in roofing talks about their most popular features," he said. "That's the F. Then everybody talks about their so-called obvious benefits — that's the B. But I keep the box of Fab handy so I never forget to talk about the A. The A is what *they* accomplish, specifically the actual advantages *they* receive from all our great roofing features and our firm. That way I always focus on and talk about specific features and the actual advantages we deliver to get them the personal benefits they want."

"Tell me more," I asked. I could see where he was going with this.

"Okay," Lorrie said. "Well . . . in reality, I really don't sell roofs. I sell things like our thirty-year warranty and how it gives them the advantage of increased home value and makes their house easier to sell when they move to Florida, or how our specialty shingles give them the advantage of warmer houses and the benefit of lower heating bills. It varies. I never know when I go in what they want to accomplish or why. They say they want a new roof. I take nothing for granted. Instead, I take the time when I'm in the house to find out what they really want and why it is important to them. Then I make sure I mention the appropriate features, talk a lot about the advantages of them and about the personal benefits. They usually turn to each other and say, 'Wow, what a great deal! This is exactly the roof we want!' Price never seems to be an issue, either, I believe because my deep discovery and my Fab approach makes the value so high the price always seems right!"

Any one of Lorrie's customers could have purchased other roofs for less. But his advantage-based approach crushed the competition and made his roof the only one to buy. He had the highest gross profit of anybody in the firm. It never ceases to amaze me what happens when you focus on the buyer and what they want to accomplish. Thank you, Lorrie, for one of the most valuable selling lessons I ever learned.

Advantage-Based Selling as the Critical Link

The advantage-based selling process Lorrie had developed instinctively is the exact, specific, tactical response every sales professional needs, regardless of what they are selling in today's world. It provides the perfect path to explain the *what* and *how* of your company and products from the customers' perspective.

When you articulate what a customer can accomplish functionally with every attribute and feature of your business, product, and service, each one can see the advantage and value of those attributes from their own perspective! By clarifying what they can actually accomplish and then personalizing the benefit, closing ratios will increase. As we mapped and analyzed this, our team realized this was the link between a compelling value promise and a successful sale. Furthermore, it answers the two big curiosity questions — what do you do and how do you do that?

We tested it internally in our own corporate sales efforts and developed a system — a matrix anyone can use to execute the advantage-based selling process brilliantly. We then began to introduce it to our clients. Regardless of the type of industry, business, product, or services the system is applied to, it has significantly elevated closing ratios at all levels of sales experience.

To help you execute this process, we invite you to use the Advantage-Based Selling Matrix in the Reader and Resources section of my website. You can download it for free. It will provide a clear path to identifying the real advantages and true benefits for each feature and attribute of your products or services. By codifying the real advantages and true benefits from the consumer's perspective in advance, you'll have a clear syllabus to execute the advantage-based selling process every time, in every sales conversation. You can simply commit each feature/attribute, advantage, and benefit to memory. Make them part of your professional sales lexicon's DNA. After deep discovery you can then select the right features/attributes and advantages and personalize the benefits to address why they want to buy your products and services.

To begin to learn and use this new language and advantage-based selling process, follow these steps:

Step 1
List six to seven important features and attributes of your business and its products or services down the left side of the matrix you downloaded or on a piece of paper. These will likely be those that are the most compelling or unique to you.

Step 2
To the right of each listed feature and attribute, write down its clear functional advantages (what it actually accomplishes functionally) for the buyer. Here is how:

- Revisit your UVP surveys, particularly the question I encouraged you to ask about what some of your features and attributes actually accomplished for your best customers and how those benefited them. Review their answers and you will discover your best customers' perceived functional advantages and emotional benefits of each feature and attribute you asked about.
- Extract their "Here is what I accomplished" answers and write them on this matrix next to the appropriate feature/attribute.
- Look carefully at answers to other questions on the UVP survey. You'll see many specific tactical phrases that your best customers used to describe what they accomplished from your business, its products, or its services. Extract those also and align them to the feature or attribute that best delivers what they said they accomplished.

Step 3
Review the "How did you benefit from it" portion of your feature/
attribute questions on your UVP survey. Right there in black and
white is their emotional benefit. List the emotional benefits they
said they received adjacent to the appropriate feature and advantage. Once you have completed this extraction process and listed
all the answers gleaned from your UVP surveys, you are well on
your way.

Step 4
Now ask yourself what other customers have told you they have
accomplished as a result of a particular feature or attribute. What
benefits have they expressed? Once you begin to work with and
recognize the language of the buyer, you'll likely make one or two
additions to your advantages and benefits for each attribute or feature from their perspective. Don't revert back to your perspective,
however. Add only if you recall their commentary or their answers
or you really can see the features from the buyers' point of view.

Step 5
You may discover as you complete the matrix that some features
and attributes have several functional advantages and emotional
benefits. Likewise, many of the advantages and benefits fit several
of the features and attributes of your business. This is not uncommon and not an issue. However, do take an objective look at your
features and attributes. What really are the best functional advantages and emotional benefits for each of them? Assign as many as
truly fit the appropriate feature or attribute. Make those your final
choices to learn and memorize.

Transitions that Sell

To ensure you get the advantage-based selling approach right every time, use these proven transitions and achieve maximum value from each one:

1. When you articulate a feature or attribute, be sure you preface the advantage with the transition before you speak to the functional advantage: "And what this means to you is . . ." This transition ensures that you get their attention.
2. State the specific functional advantage. Tell them with conviction what they will actually accomplish with the feature or attribute.
3. Follow with the second transition: "And the benefit to you is . . ." This ensures that the personalized benefit and full outcome is about to be made clear and will resonate with them.
4. State the relevant personalized benefit to them. Why does this work? Because you have captured their attention with the preface before the advantage with "And what this means to you is . . ." and further solidified the value of the advantage with, "And the benefit to you is . . ." Using this exact phraseology to transition between each feature/attribute and its advantages and benefits makes the value crystal clear because it is wholly from the customer's perspective.

Here are a couple of examples. Read them aloud so you can experience the smooth flow and how it captures a prospect's attention:

Selling Copiers
"Mr. David, we have a five-year, all-inclusive service plan and warranty on this copier [the feature/attribute], and what this means for you is [first transition] that you will not have any additional expenses for maintenance or service during the next five years [their

advantage, i.e., what they will accomplish], and the benefit to you [second transition] is that you'll enjoy worry-free and expense-free ownership [personalized benefit they are seeking]!"

Selling Siding
"Janet, our siding coloring is 10 percent thicker than required by code [the feature/attribute], and what that means to you is [first transition] that you won't have to paint your house again [the advantage, i.e., what they will accomplish], and the benefit to you is [second transition] that you will never have to budget for that expense again [personalized benefit they are seeking]!"

The Keys to Brilliant Advantage-Based Selling

To make this work for you, here are three level-setting points:

1. Be willing to accept that not only have things changed but that you will need to overcome the fear, uncertainty, and doubt that comes with a change in a sales presentation process that has worked for you in the past. But by making this change to advantage-based selling you will not only close more sales, you'll also make your work as a problem-solver even more of a pleasure.

2. Complete and utilize the Advantage-Based Selling Matrix so you'll know the appropriate and convincing functional advantages and emotional benefits of every product feature and business attribute you offer. When combined with deep discovery, this advantage-based selling process is so compelling, it inspires prospective buyers to say yes.

3. Integrate and use advantage-based selling consistently in all your sales activities. A sales manager for one of our clients called to tell me of his success in learning and adopting this new selling process. He had just

closed a large sale with an executive who had inquired about their Unique Value Promise. His opening comment when I picked up the phone was, "It works, it works, it works." Yes, advantage-based selling works, but I congratulated him because *he* was working it. The same is true for all of us. So set aside your fear, uncertainty, and doubts. Reset your sales presentation to follow the process exactly, and become fluent in this new language for this new era of opportunity.

But What About Price?

The advantage-based selling approach gives consumers what they want and thus reduces price pressure. You know from experience that when you want to buy something, if the value is high, then price is less of a factor.

While cutting prices may deliver short-term cash flow, it erodes your position and your distinctive presence with consumers. Not only that, it reduces the long-term value of your business and its products or services. If, on the other hand, you focus on discovering the specific outcomes consumers want and use the advantage-based selling process, your value and the value of your products and services to the consumer increases. It also reinforces your distinct position and presence in the marketplace.

Years of experience has shown me that when buyers are accomplishing what they want to accomplish, price is way down the list of objections or stumbling blocks. However, if you hear "the price seems high," the reason is likely because either you didn't get full discovery or your selected features and functional advantages or emotional benefits are not yet relevant or clear. So avoid getting caught up in the reduction of value by cutting the price. Instead, probe deeply and then focus on the right features and corresponding advantages that will help the buyer accomplish what they want; then lock them in with personalized benefits.

Wrap-up

This new approach:

1. Creates an unmistakable opportunity for the business and individual that utilizes deep discovery to find out the real reasons why buyers want to buy.
2. Moves those who inquire to closure by utilizing the customer-centric, advantage-based selling process.
3. Provides the proven path and right perspective (theirs) needed to be congruent with and maximize your Unique Value Promise and distinct presence in the marketplace.

ACTION POINTS

1. Would your sales cycle be shorter and your closing ratio higher if you knew even more about what "they" wanted and then used the advantage-based sales process to deliver it?
2. Have potential buyers said, "I don't know" or "I am not sure" far too often?
3. Is "the price (or fee) seems high" a common objection?
4. Are you clear on every functional advantage and emotional benefit delivered by the attributes and features of your business or its products?
5. What will you do right now to execute the advantage-based selling approach in order to be more effective and close more sales?

9

Step Six: Exceeding Expectations in Customer Service

"A business absolutely devoted to service will only have one worry about profits: they will be embarrassingly large!"
— HENRY FORD

HUNDREDS OF THOUSANDS of words have been written and read about the importance of customer service and how to create a good service platform. The number of satisfied customers (and the degree to which they are satisfied) is the typical bar by which most service platforms are measured. Although all this education and execution to create satisfied customers is well intentioned, it falls short for those who want a distinct presence in today's competitive marketplace.

Just about every business in the marketplace claims that their terrific customer service is a big reason to do business with them. From the customer's perspective, however, good customer service is what they expect to get when they make a purchase in any industry or profession. It's not the exception but the rule, so it's not the real reason why they decide to choose a particular product or service.

Whether it is an automobile, a new computer, or something as mundane as french fries at a fast-food restaurant, people expect if for any reason it doesn't meet their expectations the purchase will be made right. Thus to deliver good customer service is no longer enough. Yes, it may create satisfied customers, but in today's competitive marketplace a customer who is merely satisfied is very often still loyalty neutral.

Why Elevated Interactions and Personalized Customer Service Are Vital

Your objective shouldn't be just to have satisfied customers but rather delighted advocates for your enterprise.

A satisfied customer may have been happy with the customer service or another aspect of the products or the interaction, but nothing stands out in their mind. When asked, they tell us, "Yes, they were pretty good," or "I am usually satisfied with them." They may be satisfied but they are certainly not delighted. They don't tell others about you or your business proactively. Hearing about a competitor, finding a better price, or being given another opportunity to take their business elsewhere — they likely will.

Delighted advocates, on the other hand, give you rave reviews. They talk about the elevated experiences and personalized service they receive. They advance your enterprise constantly through their positive word of mouth. They talk about their fantastic experience and interactions with your business at every opportunity.

Here's an illustration that demonstrates the need for businesses and individuals to provide a truly unique and elevated experience for their customers if they want to be seen as a business of distinction, one that has broken away from the competition. Let's start with an acronym, PSET:

P refers to the products, platform, or process you offer to the marketplace.

S refers to the service you promote and provide to your customers.

E speaks to the elevated experience you must deliver in customer service and interactions to fortify your distinct presence.

T represents a transformed customer — the actual outcome when you elevate customer experiences with you and your business. No longer merely satisfied, but instead a delighted advocate.

Commoditization has become rampant in most industries. As you know, commoditization occurs when attributes like product specs, price, availability, service, and brand are given economic value. This occurs as a result of the constant message from nearly every enterprise about P (their products, platform, process) and S (service).

What is required to be distinct and to break away from your competition is to live out your Unique Value Promise by focusing on and consistently delivering E: an elevated experience in all your services and interactions.

When you do, the customer believes they can count on you and your promise time and time again. This consistency creates trust and credibility. In Ken Blanchard and Sheldon Bowles's book, *Raving Fans: A Revolutionary Approach to Customer Service*, the authors paint a picture of the importance of reengineering or improving these "moments of truth" when customers are in direct contact with your business.

To paraphrase Blanchard and Bowles, you need to exceed expectations each and every time the customer deals with you. When you do that, you T: transform the customer and capture their loyalty. The result: marketplace distinction and delighted advocates who are less concerned about price while — more important — they see, perceive, and receive great value from you and your business. Consequently, they tell others in the marketplace.

Some have argued only large businesses can really elevate the customer experience, or, conversely only small ones. In reality, with clear, open-minded assessment and a commitment from you and your team, any business of any size in any industry or market can elevate current customer experiences and interactions.

As an example, when my wife was recently recovering from surgery, the doctor requested she stay close to the hospital until she was well enough to travel. We stayed at the Hotel Los Gatos and Spa in Los Gatos, California. The staff there exceeded all of our expectations. From finding a room to fit her special needs to blocking all incoming calls to the room to special maid service to running errands, they went above and beyond all our expectations. I asked one of the managers how and why they did that so consistently.

"Oh, we meet regularly to find ways to anticipate and satisfy our guests' needs. We want to elevate their experience so we leave nothing to chance."

Then there was the time I needed shirts laundered one day in Port Charlotte, Florida. I stopped at The Greener Cleaner and inquired.

"Sure, they will be done by five p.m.," they said.

The challenge was, my flight was at five p.m.

No problem, they replied — "What time do you need them?"

"By three p.m., at the latest."

Their answer?

"Let's make it easy for you. We'll have them done by one o'clock and deliver them to your meeting location by one thirty."

Having never set foot in the place before, I was struck by their helpfulness and their commitment to elevate my experience.

So how about your business? What can you do to improve and elevate your customers' experience?

If you're a provider like Oceanic Time Warner Cable in Hawaii, can you set a two-hour window instead of just "morning or afternoon" slots for when your service technician will arrive? Can your technicians call twenty minutes before they arrive to inform your customer they will be there shortly—as Oceanic does?

These little things create a portfolio of memorable and elevated experiences for your customers. As you assess your current service and interaction platform, you'll discover many opportunities. By elevating service and customer interactions, you can fortify your distinct presence and demonstrate you truly are customer-centric. It also demonstrates your commitment to deliver on your Unique Value Promise every day in every way.

Creating Your Own Delighted Advocates

Creating elevated customer experiences and service doesn't happen overnight. The road to distinction requires that you thoroughly assess your entire service and customer interaction platform. By first determining where you are now and then figuring out what you can do to elevate those interactions and experiences, you'll be on the right track to living out your promise and creating advocates. Use your Unique Value Promise as your guide. This is who you are and what you want to be known for in the marketplace. Assess every nuance of customer service and interface you have currently, from how the telephone is answered to how the customer is cultivated after the sale. Realize that by making small changes each and every day, week, and month, you'll gradually achieve a consistent elevated experience for all customers.

To ensure that the changes you need to make are clear and that they get made, bring in your promise integration teams as described in Chapter 6. Ask them to look at your service and customer interactions and evaluate each as though they were *your* customer. Let them know everything is on the table. Ask them what things need to be elevated and improved. Then empower them to take action to make the adjustments that are needed. Use the ninety-day plan template I offered earlier to get the incremental changes implemented. It's free in the Reader Resources section of my website. List even the smallest items you can improve upon to live out your promise every day and provide an elevated experience for all.

Revisiting Fundamentals

Here are specific, proven tactics you and your business can use to seed the process of elevating customer experiences and service interactions. Use this foundational list and work with your team to create many more techniques that are specific to your business.

To help you build and execute these more easily, I've listed them as separate tactics. Approach each with an open mind and the creative energy to utilize them in your business. Most importantly, read these with your customers' perspective in mind.

Tactic 1: When a customer walks into a store, office, or lobby, they should be greeted. There is nothing quite like feeling welcomed. Not with the usual "Can I help you?" but instead a "Welcome to [your store or business name]," which is far more inviting and elevated.

For example, Waffle House, the ubiquitous Southern restaurant, gets it right every time. The minute you walk in the door at one of their sixteen hundred-plus locations open 24/7, it's "Welcome to Waffle House" from the whole team working that shift. A warm greeting sets the tone for a successful interaction and dining experience.

I was recently at a Walgreens in Scottsdale, Arizona, and had that same experience: a warm greeting and pleasant smile. In contrast, "Can I help you?" sets the stage for "No, just looking." Following this exchange, most consumers live up to it by glancing around aimlessly and finding an exit before they find what they might in fact have been looking for.

Be sure everyone on your team puts out the welcome mat. As customers look through the store, walk through the office, or wait in the lobby, every team member they come into contact with should say, "Good morning," "Good afternoon," or "Good evening." The people who work for distinctive hotels and restaurants are taught this from day one. Even the housekeepers are taught to stop what they are doing and greet you when you pass them in the hall. You can elevate your customers' experience by doing the same, whether you're a very small business or a large corporation. If you do, you'll demonstrate and extend a culture that is gracious, warm, and friendly. It's so seldom practiced, it immediately sets their experience with you apart from all others.

Tactic 2: After you've met, always use the customer's name. It generates a sense of belonging and personalizes the experience. If you don't remember their name, say "Please pronounce or spell your name so I have it correct." This is far better than, "Can you remind me what your name is?" If needed, spell it out phonetically in your database so everyone who accesses it pronounces it right — every time.

Tactic 3: Be aware of your public spaces. Why? First impressions in your store, shop, or office set customers on the pathway to seeing you as distinct. With this in mind, check to see what your front door or waiting room looks like at first glance. Is it organized or chaotic? Is it exceptional or just acceptable? Many business owners recognize the importance of this first impression and work hard to make customers comfortable in lobbies, showrooms, even service department waiting rooms. Here are a few proven tips businesses can use to create a distinctive experience and first impression for their customers in their public spaces:

- Be sure reading materials are recent and appropriate. No matter what your business, avoid magazines that are out of date, dog-eared or shabby, lurid, sensational, or in bad taste. Elevate the tone with recently published, tastefully designed, and easy-to-read magazines or newsletters that are appropriate to your particular community or target market.

- Provide a fresh beverage, offered graciously. Coffee, tea, cold water, or soda elevates the interactions and experiences. Avoid convenience-store style cups. If it looks like Styrofoam, it probably is! In professional and corporate offices, china cups and saucers provide an elevated surprise. In repair shops, inexpensive mugs with the business name and value promise emblazoned on them work great, particularly if you encourage people to take those mugs home. They serve as subtle reminders and great conversation starters for your delighted advocates when their neighbors ask, "Where did you get that?" or "What do you know about that company?"
- Be sure you display your Unique Value Promise in your public areas as a reminder to all of what makes you distinct.
- Be sure your public areas are clean and inviting. No plastic chairs, dim lights, chipped paint, peeling wallpaper, or threadbare carpets. Your restrooms should be inspected hourly for soap, hand sanitizer, hand towels, and other necessities, and must be spotlessly clean. How many of us have been to a restaurant or service station or convenience store and haven't gone back because of the impression we received from a restroom visit?

Tactic 4: Good telephone etiquette is crucial. Anyone who answers the phone should respond to questions with a tone of warm interest and concern — never just going through the motions or, worse, expressing annoyance. For many people, the first point of contact, particularly in a nonretail environment, is the telephone. Incoming calls often are an interruption in a busy office. Nevertheless, it's vital that everyone who talks with a customer should have a smile in their voice and be friendly.

Even a busy receptionist (whom we refer to as the Director of

First Impressions) must be on guard and be aware of the attitude and image they're creating from their tone of voice.

When I was head of sales and marketing for the *Robb Report,* every employee who answered calls or interfaced with the client had a mirror on their desk. Why? To be sure they smiled on every call. It was Mahatma Gandhi who said, "Life is like a mirror; if I smile, the mirror returns the smile. The same attitude I have towards life is what life will have towards me."

Speaking of a smile, if you want to elevate customer experience, by all means avoid automated answering systems. We've all heard the robotic voice listing seventeen options that you can't possibly remember and then a maze of endless further options to navigate through before you can actually speak to a real person. This automated, depersonalized response has become ubiquitous and it's a terrible idea. No one who wants to have exceptional customer service should have such a system in their organization. And consumers know you're "saving money" — at their expense!

To elevate customer interaction be sure the telephone is answered by an individual by the third ring. In today's "I want it now" world, responsiveness is rarely found and yet is nevertheless anxiously sought after by consumers. It is why many hotels today have one number to call or button to push to get quick service. It eliminates the endless ringing phone when calling room service or housekeeping.

It's essential to have a uniform enterprise-wide greeting that reinforces a desire to help and at the same time creates a positive impression. For example: "Thank you for calling Citigroup. This is Melissa. How may I help you?"

Another example of how this question can drive sales, even when asked by non-salespeople, is Walmart. They increased sales volume by changing the question of inquiry on their employees' smocks from "May I help you?" to "How may I help you?" No longer can you respond with a simple yes or no. Now you feel compelled to tell them how they can help. The same is true when answering the telephone. It encourages customers to tell their story and feel a sense of meaning and significance when calling with an inquiry.

Transfer graciously. If it's necessary to move the call to another department or team member, say "May I place you on hold while I connect you?" Or, "One moment, please, while I connect you." Or, if there is uncertainty whether or not the person is available, say "May I place you on hold while I locate them?" As fundamental as this may seem, our experience is that very few administrative personnel have been taught this or use it.

How many times have you been told to "hang on" or "let me see if she wants to talk to you" or "if they're taking calls"? Or the experience I had recently when the response was "He never tells me where he's going!"

Delightful. Almost as good as "Let me see if I can find where he's hiding."

Be sure people are positioned positively if they have to say someone is unavailable to take a call or inquiry. An acceptable and helpful response, such as "He's on another call—how may I help you?" or "She's currently working with another customer," is a far cry from the unacceptable and unprofessional "He's out closing a big sale" or "She's meeting with an unhappy customer."

You get the idea. Position unavailability positively and elevate the customer's perception of the people and the organization.

Avoid sending callers straight to voicemail—a very cold and frustrating experience that we've all had. Instead, always answer the phone, then offer an elevated and personalized interaction. Conventional service might say something like "He's in a meeting, would you like his voicemail?" Instead, demonstrate a willingness to serve: "He's in a team meeting. How may I help you?" Most people respond enthusiastically to this humanized, personal approach versus the dehumanization they feel with automated voicemail. To be distinct—do what others don't do!

If you're unable to help, set a telephone appointment. We all dislike phone tag, so change the game. Everyone should provide their support staff access to their calendar. Why? Scheduling a telephone appointment for the return call immediately elevates the customer's experience and sense of service. It demonstrates a well-organized, customer-focused organization.

We've found this kind of language works very well: "She's working with another customer but could call you back today between two and four p.m. Let's set a telephone appointment during that time. What time works best for you?"

Tactic 5: When your interaction is complete, escort your customers out. In professional firms such as legal, accounting, real estate, or financial services, ride down the elevator with them or walk with them to the lobby. In retail stores, walk them to the door.

Why? It demonstrates that you're never too busy for them. And, they may also tell you things that might not have emerged in your office or on the sales floor. Sometimes it's those final exchanges that turn out to be the most valuable for everyone.

Speaking of ending on a positive note, furnish customers with umbrellas, if needed, for inclement weather. I was recently at a prospective client's office in Charlotte, North Carolina. The garage was across the street from the building. It was raining hard and I watched their clients run to the garage without an umbrella. My first thought was to wonder why the business didn't provide umbrellas with their name and UVP to every client leaving that day. How good would it be to know that every rainy day, people were marketing their business all over town?

Tactic 6: Confirm all appointments in advance. Many businesses do this now, but too many others don't. Whether you are a medical or legal firm, a personal trainer, a repair shop, or a home service, reaching out to confirm appointments goes a long way toward creating delighted advocates and business efficiency.

When it's appropriate, you can also send agendas in advance for meetings with individuals that will require research or entail multiple topics—for example, an attorney's offices, financial services, real estate, and so forth. An agenda in advance helps every client prepare for the meeting.

However, the first item on every agenda should always be: What are the three things you want to discuss at this meeting? Any meeting or any conversation with any customer should always be about them. It doesn't matter if you don't complete the items on your agenda, as long as they complete theirs. If they do, it elevates their experience and reinforces your distinctive presence.

Tactic 7: Focus on personal touches that make a difference. The little things are usually what people remember most. Every business should have a database of every customer's and prospect's name and contact information. In addition, you should store such things as their first purchase date or account anniversaries; business, profession, or employment start dates; children's accomplishments (i.e., graduation, marriage, etc.), as well as their special interests. This information is vitally important as it can be used to cultivate customers and build knowledge about prospective customers on an ongoing basis.

Some retailers get this right every time. They send special notes to customers on their special days, and advance notices of store events and special customer activities. No matter what type of business you are in, knowing who your customers and prospects are is important. Acting on that knowledge will set you apart.

Tactic 8: Create and continually update a new-customer "owner's manual" specific for your local/regional customers. Not the standard manufacturer's owner's manual but rather one personalized for them. Contents could include who to contact specifically in your organization for service, parts, billing, product info, trouble-shooting, or general information and inquiries.

Why? To ensure easy interface and an elevated experience for the consumer.

Tactic 9: Always set realistic time frames and clear deliverables to be sure you create delighted advocates. The old cliché about under-promising and over-delivering remains viable because it has withstood the test of time. However, if you are about to miss a deadline or deliverable, the key is to act proactively, not reactively. If a product or service is going to be late, call in advance of the due date or time. Avoid waiting until after the expected time to alert the customer.

If you reach out to reset expectations and give a clear reason for your miss, most people are understanding. Calling after, or worse, waiting for them to call you, is seen only as poor service and just a bad excuse.

Tactic 10: Always do what you say you will do because nothing, absolutely nothing destroys trust or confidence in a business more readily than not following through. Having a Unique Value Promise gives you a distinct presence, but keeping your word reinforces that you are a business and organization of distinction.

Tactic 11: Elevating and exceeding customer expectations is an ongoing process. Listen constantly for customer requests and capture them so you can continually elevate your service and interactions.

Knowing what your customers want and need is critical to always being on the cutting edge of service and communication. Meet with your team no less often than monthly to debrief and brainstorm with them on possible action points that will create more delighted advocates. Look for ways to break bottlenecks in processes and shipping. Create and set protocols to repair breakdowns in communications and responsiveness. Probe for solutions to areas of demonstrated or perceived customer discomfort or inconvenience. Be relentless in your desire to incrementally elevate your customers' experiences, service, and interactions with your business.

Tactic 12: To deliver a constant flow of creative steps that will elevate service and interactions, be sure to put them in writing.

Write all your elevated service and experience protocols into your policy and procedures manual and educational coursework. The point is not just to have them written down somewhere, it's to make all of your expectations known to every individual currently in your organization and to those who will join in the future. Most importantly, continually educate every member of your team so they have the knowledge and confidence to elevate every interaction and service. Educate not once, not twice, but on an ongoing basis—just as the Ritz-Carlton does. Also, we have many clients who send short e-mail reminders to their team members every week on a different and specific protocol they use to elevate interactions and service.

Remember: out of sight, out of business. Your objective is to protect and grow your distinct presence in the marketplace. It will happen if you constantly reinforce your promise with elevated experiences and service deliverables. Which brings us to our final tactic.

Tactic 13: In addition to your policy and procedures manual and educational coursework, publish your own internal Service Values Guide and make it available to everyone in your organization.

Here is ours:

My Service Values for Successful Client Relationships

1. I will always be aware that clients are counting on me.
2. I will get to know each client personally and create valued clients for life.
3. I will seek to provide guidance in all situations.
4. I will use humor when under pressure.
5. I will not speak negatively of anyone—ever.
6. I will never display anger.
7. I will respond to all communications immediately, whenever and wherever possible.

8. I will protect the privacy and security of all clients and their issues at all times.

9. I will be friendly and approachable and continually seek to exceed my clients' expectations.

10. I will place the client's interest first above the firm's providing it is an ethical request.

Wrap-up

What has come to mind as you've reviewed these tactics? Have you thought about how you can elevate service and personalize every customer interaction as a part of your promise and resultant culture?

There are many things you and your promise-integration teams can do to elevate every touch point and deliver elevated experiences to your customers.

As an example: If you're running a hair salon specializing in cutting children's hair, could you be celebrating kids' birthdays, or hosting monthly parties? How about their bar mitzvahs or bat mitzvahs, or first communions?

If you own or run a plumbing company, could your technicians wear disposable booties in customers' houses? It shows respect and subtly demonstrates you care. Could you send along a personal thank-you note with the bill after a repair? How about thoughtful reminders of areas of household or commercial plumbing that need annual service? Could it include services the property owner can do on their own? To communicate that, you truly have their best interest at heart!

If you are the head of communications or compliance for a major business, could you adjust communications protocols so that your sales and service teams correspond with customers and prospects more effectively and in a personal way? Not only to reinforce your promise, but to let the customer know they matter as individuals, not just as a revenue provider! Or if you own or manage a restaurant, could you make available phone-charging cables for your guests?

Think and work creatively and collaboratively. You'll find it easier to reset your vision of what elevated experience, service, and interaction really is and can be for your organization, and you will win where others lose, and succeed where others fail.

ACTION POINTS

1. Are you committed to elevating your service and all customer interactions?
2. Do your current interactions create the impression that you are exceptional and organized?
3. What specific incremental steps can you take right now to transform satisfied customers into delighted advocates?

10

Tales from the Front Lines

'VE LEARNED OVER the years that nothing teaches better than a good story. So I've gone through my archives and personal notes to find some exemplary case histories that show the Power of Why in action.

What follows are four stories about our work with some very different organizations and their unique needs:

1. A large financial firm that was having trouble acquiring and retaining new wealth-management clients.
2. Kelron Logistics, a transportation management company whose margins were under pressure, sales were suffering, and leadership needed to step up to a new level.
3. Mount Paran Church of God, a large Pentecostal church that was having problems finding the funding they needed to meet the needs of their multi-campus parishioners.
4. The Conklin Company, a manufacturing and distribution operation determined to grow their distribution system of independent business operators.

I think you'll find each of them shows a different application of the Power of Why and how the methods in this book can work for you and your enterprise.

The Upscale Financial Firm

I received a call from a well-known financial advisory firm that wishes to remain anonymous. They told me they were concerned about how they were viewed in the marketplace by the affluent and wealthy.

"What's the problem?" I asked them.

"Well, one of our best clients introduced us to a friend of his with a high net worth, just the kind of fellow that we're targeting for increasing our business. This gentleman told us that he was 'somewhat satisfied' with his existing firm but 'willing to explore other options.'"

"Sounds good so far."

"Right. We had a great introduction from our friend and then had what we thought was a good meeting. But then: a big shock. We got this one-line e-mail: 'Thank you, but we have a ten-year relationship with our existing firm and see no value in moving our portfolio to you.'"

"Wow," I said. "A rare moment of candor in what's usually a nondescript business communication." I thought for a moment, then asked them, "Why *should* someone do business with you?"

Their response was all about their attributes and how they did things — their years of experience, proven investment platform, education, and good service. What they didn't realize is that they weren't addressing the most important questions this prospect (and every other) was actually asking: "Why should I change firms? What can your firm do for me?" Unfortunately, they lost an opportunity because they answered his "why" question with *who* they are, *what* they have, and *how* they do things. They didn't offer any clarity on what they would actually accomplish for the prospective client.

"Listen," I explained. "As important and exciting as your qualifications and process might be to you, it's essential that you understand what prospective clients really want to accomplish."

I pointed out that at a strategic level, the reasons they gave to do business with them were firm-centric, not consumer outcome–centric. They weren't thinking from the prospect's perspective.

By this time, they were listening very carefully. "You're right. We've been experiencing very little growth lately. People just don't seem to be inquiring like they used to, and even when they do, they're not always buying. This last e-mail rejection was shocking, but consistent with a general decline. What we've been doing for years just isn't working anymore. We've got to come up with some new techniques."

I advised them that this falloff wasn't just about their sales technique. Rather, they needed to understand at a deep level *why* people inquired and what it took ultimately for them to purchase their services.

As a result of this conversation, we engaged with this firm, starting out with a two-day retreat with their entire leadership team and top support staff. We probed deeply into what they felt was their purpose as a firm. Not their vision or mission, but rather their purpose. We discussed and evaluated their way of doing business, their sales process, their client service interaction, and their culture. Several outcomes became clear:

- No one had the same answer regarding purpose.
- They offered a range of reasons to buy from them:
  * We are smart.
  * We are experienced.
  * We are ethical.
  * We manage money for people like them.

* We have a great investment model.
* We give great service.
- Their sales process was oriented to these same features and attributes.
- There was no mention of the functional or emotional outcomes clients were actually receiving, such as solving, experiencing, enjoying, clarifying, and so on.
- Their service platform was consistent but decidedly not elevated.

After this discovery and educational retreat the firm's leadership realized that in order to break out and grow they needed to re-engineer their thinking and approach. Instead of working under pressure, they needed to work from a congruent purpose. Instead of answering the prospective buyer's "why" with who they are, what they have, or how they do it, they needed to know, communicate, and deliver solely from the client's perspective.

We showed them how crucial it was for them to have true clarity about why existing clients were doing business with them, and not just at a surface level. They further realized that obtaining clarity would profoundly influence their sense of purpose, their discovery process, their marketing and sales messaging, service deliverables, and the underlying culture.

We provided them with our proprietary best-customer survey documents and engaged them in an extensive process of client interviews and discovery. Out of that experience, we uncovered the real reasons why their best clients were really doing business with them. They said things like, "You help us feel secure about our financial future . . . You always provide sound advice . . . We feel like you always pinpoint or identify clear strategies." After many client interviews and the compilation of their actual words and phrases, we helped them craft their firm's UVP.

When clients were polled, they agreed overwhelmingly that this clearly described the outcome they were receiving.

With their promise in place, we also helped them integrate their UVP into all marketing activities and prospect and client communications. It had to become a part of their corporate DNA. Consequently, we reformatted their sales process to utilize trilogy questions for deep discovery and coupled that with the use of the advantage-based selling process so that inquiries driven by their UVP actually resulted in sales. Working with the firm, we engaged in an examination of roles and responsibilities to ensure full cultural integration of their promise.

The result is that the entire organization is now working on-purpose to deliver on their promise every day and in every way. Most importantly, they are customer-centric, and inquiries and sales reflect what occurs when you plug into the Power of Why.

Their very first month after this process was completed they brought in $160 million in new assets. This velocity continues. When any member of their organization is asked, "Why should I do business with you?" he or she replies with their UVP. The prospect's response is "How do you do that?"

The Power of Why in action lets curiosity trump convincing.

Kelron Logistics

Keith Matthews and his partner Geoff Bennett founded their transportation management company, Kelron Logistics, in 1992. I had coached and mentored many of the young guns in the province of Ontario who wanted to "do their own thing" during those years. Keith and Geoff started the company with an excellent offering and hit the ground running, full of enthusiasm and the traditional exuberance of young entrepreneurs.

They started in Geoff's basement in Mississauga, a suburb of Toronto, and within a year had rented office space. Their sales grew and they added employees. Within three years, they built a marketing platform and a sales system, and moved into larger facilities in Toronto. Business was booming and their initial goal to do $40 million by the time they each were forty was well realized.

They expanded to the United States in 2000, bought a ware-house business in 2001, and spearheaded their transportation management business in 2005. Sales were now closing in on $80 million annually. They opened more offices both in Canada and the United States and landed a large single-source transportation management contract in 2007 with LG Electronics in Canada.

Keith's responsibilities had always been in the company's sales and marketing effort and Geoff's involved the operating and financial aspects of the business. Life was good! They were riding the wave, so to speak. Their business culture began to have "swagger" and they made the decision to rebrand around their success. Kelron's rebranding, developed with the help of an ad agency in 2007, demonstrated their level of confidence in their unique selling proposition: "Intelligent Transportation Delivered."

Unbeknownst to them, however, there were some serious problems looming in the economy and in their business that no one in their company recognized or foresaw. In fiscal 2010, challenges began to emerge. Their margins were under pressure, they had high turnover in sales, their staff was asking questions, and most importantly, the focus was on Geoff and Keith to step up with a new level of leadership.

I got a call from Keith on February 28, 2012. After I asked him some questions about Kelron's sales and marketing, I began to describe a discovery my team and I had made in buyer behavior since the crash of 2008. He said it was a "revelation" and engaged us immediately to focus on creating the right message and sales focus to help Kelron capture new customers.

Keith and his people provided us with all of their recently completed customer research data. We immediately identified the changes and new path they needed to take to regain their momentum. We showed them that success today was not about their attributes such as who or how good they were. Rather, it was first understanding, then communicating and delivering, solely and wholly from the buyer's perspective.

As a result, we held extensive meetings with their leadership team, including the top salespeople. During the next phase we showed them:

1. Why it wasn't just believing they understood the buyer's perspective, but truly re-engineering the way they thought.

2. How to craft three potential value promises using the exact words their best customers used to describe what they received from Kelron both functionally and emotionally.

3. That they needed to circle back to those best customers they had originally interviewed. When they presented the choices to each of them to vote on, something magical began to emerge. The process allowed them to talk with their best customers in a completely different way. Many of them were honored that they'd been asked to participate in what would become a new beginning for the company. The process crystallized the Kelron team's thinking that they were all on the right path to break out in a very competitive marketplace.

4. That this process clearly demonstrated how their sales would increase if their best customers, not Kelron, decided what the message and promise of value should be. Once all of the votes were tallied, they had a clear winner and their new promise of value was born, which paved the way for the next chapter in their business.

Keith and Geoff scheduled meetings at every one of Kelron's locations in Canada and the United States to deliver the new promise personally to everyone on their team.

"Our now clear understanding of what we accomplish for our customers and why that is important to them has made a dramatic impact on our business," Keith told me. "Our company's positioning and purpose has made a one-hundred-eighty-degree shift from being about us to being about them." It was the Power of Why in action.

"You and your team walked us through a step-by-step process that has completely revamped our marketing messages, promotion activities, and sales processes. We are elevating every service and interaction touch point with customers to make sure they're not just satisfied but delighted. Culturally our entire operation is now working with a sense of purpose—delivering on our promise to our customers and prospective customers. This is far different than our previous working under pressure for the bottom line."

The Mount Paran Church

Nonprofits that are purpose-driven also need to be aware of and communicate within the perspective of their constituent group. One such case we had the privilege of working with was the Mount Paran Church of God in Atlanta, Georgia. Founded in 1918 as the Church of God, it was the first organized Pentecostal church in Atlanta. Over the next fifty years, it had grown to seven hundred members. Dr. Paul Walker assumed the pastorate in 1960 and the church grew to ninety-five hundred members in less than twenty years.

As they rapidly grew out of their existing facilities, Mount Paran purchased an older church on sixty-five acres in north Atlanta. They renovated the property over several years, built a separate campus, and became one church in two locations.

As the economy slowed, however, ministry demands increased, ongoing mortgage payments on the new north campus became difficult, and the need to renovate the original facility loomed large. Despite having a church congregation that was known for its charitable largesse and tithing, Dr. Walker faced a dilemma: how to raise millions of dollars outside of the normal giving patterns of his parishioners to accomplish everything that needed to be done.

Dr. Walker had never felt comfortable asking for money. He had always relied on the providence of God and the dedication of his congregation. Both of his churches were increasing their membership, but any additional fundraising would be a monumental task that he felt very uneasy about undertaking, even though there was such a critical need. Consequently, he created a committee of elders, headed by his executive pastor, to explore options.

The committee decided to hire a well-qualified parishioner to be their financial consultant and planner for the campaign. Responding to the slowing economy, they decided to raise only enough to pay off the mortgage on the north property and just do needed repairs to the original campus. They created a fundraising theme around "paying off the debt and preparing for the future."

The executive pastor and financial consultant created a plan to announce the special campaign, and led the committee efforts to spread the word and pull in the contributions. Meanwhile Dr. Walker would continue doing what he did like no one else: preach incredible sermons and provide compassionate counseling. He would not, however, participate directly in fundraising according to this plan.

During this time, I had a home in Atlanta and was a regular at the Mount Paran Sunday services. Paul Walker and I had become good friends and met several times a year for lunch and fellowship. I benefited greatly from his warmth, keen insight, and inspiring biblical messages.

One cold February evening, I was in New York making final preparations for a presentation I was to deliver at a conference the next morning, when Dr. Walker called me.

"I apologize for bothering you at such a late hour, Richard, but I want your advice on a soon-to-be-announced capital campaign."

"Of course, Paul," I responded. "After all you've given me, I'm eager to see what I can do to be helpful to you and Mount Paran."

Paul said he was beginning to feel "uncomfortable about this new campaign and not sure that we're going about it in the right way."

I was somewhat surprised. He was such a confident, charismatic individual with legendary leadership skills and the gift of discernment. I asked him why there was a need for a campaign in the first place.

"We have to pay off the north campus mortgage and make some badly needed repairs to the old place."

"So what's the problem, Paul?"

After listening to his explanation, it was clear that his concerns were valid. He felt that his parishioners would be reluctant to make a substantial donation just to pay off debt.

"There isn't any emotional reward," he said. "It's all on paper. Not only that," he went on, "the people I've spoken to feel that doing critically needed repairs would beg the question. Why should we plan on only doing repairs when it's clear we need more parking, more Sunday school rooms, and with five services on Sunday, a bigger sanctuary at the original campus.

"Also, the north campus is nearly brand new and the mortgage is on that campus. So although both congregations would be participating in the campaign, the folks whose church needs the most pressing repairs would see most of their giving go to pay off the north mortgage. So in reality they would benefit the least."

I suggested that before the official launch of the campaign, we do a retreat with the committee, the pastoral staff, and Paul himself.

Three weeks later, we met for a day and a half in Stone Mountain, Georgia. My team and I led a deep expository of the genesis of the campaign and what the elders and pastors really wanted to accomplish. Early responses were about paying off the debt and making repairs. But after we divided people into small groups and probed more deeply, we discovered that they really wanted to reach more people in the Atlanta area, invest in ministering to others, and even open new locations!

Okay. Now we were getting deeper. With this new vision about what they really wanted, and why, we went to work. We explained that the campaign needed to take this message to the parishioners and present it entirely from the grassroots perspective. Furthermore, everyone needed to participate, including Dr. Walker as senior pastor. His eloquence and charisma would be the most effective way to convey this new and deeper purpose for the campaign.

Then my team and I conducted one more crucial event: we privately polled each member of the committee and pastorate at the retreat about why they personally would give to a campaign that paid off all debt, rebuilt the original campus, and also fulfilled their new vision of reaching more people and opening new locations.

We received many answers to the question that included words like, "I would give because it would help us reach more people; build for the future; raise up the next generations . . ."

That inspired us to create a capital campaign that was branded with these words in the form of the Unique Value Promise "Let Us Rise Up & Build." This biblical-style language made a strong association to scriptures central to their beliefs as a church. We then created a step-by-step plan and process to help them gain support for the campaign among parishioners at both locations. We focused on how each of them could rise up and build this vision together.

There were many moving parts to our campaign now. Pastors met in homes each week with small groups of parishioners to explain how their participation would allow them to rise up and build. To paint the big picture, members of the church affiliated with Georgia Tech created an online virtual visual tour of what they would build together, including the new facility on the original campus.

At the same time, Dr. Walker and his wife held small dinners with traditional large tithers and donors to the church, and used them to describe how they were instrumental to the plan's fulfill-ment. The executive pastor delivered bimonthly updates at both campuses. Both campuses' congregations modeled great faith and commitment to undertake the challenge and continued to grow the church during the process.

It worked. The mortgage was paid off and the entire reconstruction campaign was completed in three phases over just six years.

Raising north of $30 million during difficult economic times is a true testament to the faith of these parishioners. It's also a testament to what can happen when you have the answers from the Power of Why process to make a promise that people want to become reality in their lives.

The Conklin Company

The Conklin Company is a manufacturing and distribution operation that has been in business for over forty years. As a direct-sales company, they're known for marketing and selling their products through a network of independent business owners.

Direct selling can be best described as the marketing of products and services directly to consumers in a face-to-face manner. These transactions are generally in their homes or at their workplace and other places that aren't permanent retail locations. Direct sales typically occur through explanation or personal demonstration by an independent, direct salesperson. These salespersons are commonly referred to as direct sellers.

At the core of the Conklin business are their quality products — more than 130 across six major divisions: agronomics, animal products, building products, health, and home and vehicle products. The diversity in their product lines has given them tremendous opportunities for sales to a variety of customers.

Customers rely on Conklin's products to protect their most precious assets — their health, homes, vehicles, pets, equipment, and buildings. And because they perform time after time, customers come back again and again.

Under the tutelage and leadership of the founder, Harry Conklin, the company enjoyed modest growth until his death in 1991. In 1992, the company was purchased from the Conklin family by Charles and Judy Herbster, who at the time were one of Conklin's top independent business owners. They spent the next decade and a half adding to the product line and recruiting and developing their distribution sales force.

Even though they were enjoying reasonable growth, it was clear to them that something had to change if they were going to be seen and accepted as a fresh and new opportunity for independent business owners. Very few old-line direct-sales companies make this transition and are able to experience major increases in today's consumer-centric world.

Charles reached out to me about appearing at their annual meeting through a mutual friend in the entertainment business. We agreed to meet in San Diego at another conference where I was speaking to discuss what he wanted me to address at his event. We hit it off immediately. But it quickly became clear to me that Conklin's failure to grow sales more rapidly at the distributor level was significantly influenced by the company's overall corporate structure.

The Conklin Company was organized by product line, each headed by a "marketing" manager who was really a merchandiser disguised as a marketer. Merchandisers focus primarily on products, pricing, and packaging. Marketers typically focus on brand/product awareness, developing customer relationships, and opportunities for cross-selling opportunities.

This type of structural problem is not uncommon in many businesses. Some banks have credit-card departments that establish your new account, but the same bank's wealth-investment division is siloed separately, so very little sharing of clients or cross-selling can occur. Real estate agents may sell or help you buy a piece of property, but the mortgage specialist who works for the same company (but in another office or department) doesn't get to sell you a mortgage.

Cross-selling products and services to existing customers is a vital part of profitable growth and customer retention. I felt that removing these silos in the Conklin Company would not only promote cross-selling but move their independent distributors into a more holistic customer-centered discovery approach and sales process, as opposed to the very product-centric approach they had been using for so many years.

Finally, the organization, then headquartered in Minneapolis, needed to be revamped so that both Charles and Judy, who were living in Kansas City, could play key roles and lead the organizational changes, not just be perceived by some at corporate as "the owners."

After I spoke at their annual meeting, Charles, Judy, and I began to have discussions in earnest around these topics. The direct-sales industry can be robust in good and bad economic times, providing you make it easy for independent business owners to succeed. After a series of discussions and consultations, they acted on their instincts and followed our advice.

To fulfill their promise of "making a difference in people's lives with our products and business opportunity" they took major steps to align the organization and deliver consistently on that promise. Their driving objective was to build a company and culture committed to growth and to helping people see who they are and the difference they can make. We worked alongside them as they took many steps, including:

1. Removing the marketing managers and flattening the organization so that cross-selling and communication was not only easy but encouraged.

2. Building recognition programs that were not only

product-line-specific, but created enterprise-wide recognition as well, in competition with other distributors
regardless of products.

3. Crafting a stronger Web and social media presence to
reach potential new distributors, and to better support
existing ones.

4. Reviewing every aspect of their organization to uncover areas that needed to be improved in their distributors' experience with corporate and other distributors,
then working internally to get those issues owned and
handled by those responsible.

5. Improving their training processes to include a state-
of-the-industry leadership educational program for
their new and existing independent business owners.
Their sales training was revamped to ensure deep customer discovery by the independent distributors so
that cross-sell opportunities were revealed and successfully concluded.

6. Making the really tough decision to move the headquarters to Kansas City in the middle of all these other
changes. Manufacturing would remain in Minneapolis,
but distributor support and internal operations were
moved to the new headquarters and, after a period of
transition and further reorganization, Judy became
(and remains) the head of that organization.

Judy has instilled in every employee the idea that their one and
only focus is to make their core promise a reality for every distributor through exemplary service and personalized support.
Charles has focused his efforts on what he does best: recruiting,
training, and distributor relations. He spends many, many weeks
on the road meeting with their independent business owners to
help them grow their businesses.

These were all difficult decisions that required the Herbsters to re-engineer the business and no longer rely on what had made the Conklin Company successful prior to their taking over the business. Rather, they were willing participants in our consultations and were committed to learning and taking the next step on the road to elevated performance.

This meant that they didn't just adopt so-called industry "best practices," but engaged with us to create the right practices for their business. In the end they have made the dramatic shift from a merchandising organization to a marketing organization. No longer focused solely on products, they're now paying a lot of attention to the people who ultimately sell their great products.

Net result?

In a very difficult economic environment, the Conklin Company has grown from just over $20 million in sales to well over $100 million, and they now have a vast network of independent sales owners distributing their products throughout the United States.

• • •

My hope is that these stories resonate with you and encourage you to break out in your competitive marketplace by putting the Power of Why into action.

EPILOGUE
Go Forth and Knock 'Em Alive

"Let go of your attachment to being right, and suddenly your mind is more open."
— RALPH MARSTON, AUTHOR OF *THE POWER OF TEN BILLION DREAMS*

WE'VE REACHED THE END of our journey together. It's been a privilege to share with you the way to an elevated business performance in today's marketplace. I hope that by now you totally understand the Power of Why and have accomplished whatever goal inspired you to buy this book in the first place. This process will help you approach your problems and do things very differently.

The times they are a-changin', no doubt about it. Being just somewhat visible to potential customers is no longer enough. It's critical that you break out and be seen as distinct from all the other businesses and purchase options consumers are choosing from today.

As good as your business may be from your perspective, consumers are hungry for a business that understands, communicates, and delivers from *their* perspective. To create a distinct presence requires changing the way you see and do things. Trumpeting your attributes and features can no longer be the main thrust of your promotion. Instead, you must recognize the power that comes from knowing the real reasons why people inquire and ultimately purchase from your business.

This key component of distinction requires engaging with your best customers and listening carefully to what they say they value. You'll no longer be using a unique selling proposition to convince people to buy. Rather, you'll craft and use a Unique Value Promise that compels people to inquire and engage in a purchase conversation.

Now that you're promising customers a new level of psychologically and emotionally satisfying outcomes, you have to meet their expectations every time. As you develop a promise-centric culture, your team must be equipped to deliver. With your promise in place and your team on board, you'll be ready to take your place of distinction in the marketplace. This requires that every customer and prospective customer communication and touch point carries your Unique Value Promise into the marketplace.

The curiosity driven by your UVP will lead to more business, but only if your sales team makes the changes necessary to stay congruent with its customer-centric promotion. By probing deeply with trilogy questions, they'll discover what people want to accomplish with your products and services. When they combine that insight with advantage-based selling, the results will convert increased inquiries into increased sales.

Your objective is to never again blend in. To sustain your breaking away from the pack in a competitive marketplace, it's essential that you elevate your service and customer interactions so that you no longer just have satisfied clients, but delighted advocates instead.

"Those who cannot change their minds cannot change
anything."
— GEORGE BERNARD SHAW

If I've done my part correctly, this famous quotation doesn't ap-
ply to you, the reader of this book. You've already had a change of
mind and are compelled and committed to accomplish your goals.

Good fortune and blessing to us all.

Further Study and Inspiration

BOOKS

Blue Ocean Strategy: How to Create Uncontested Market Space and Make Competition Irrelevant by W. Chan Kim and Renée Mauborgne
Brand: It Ain't the Logo* (*It's What People Think of You) by Ted Matthews
How to Win Friends and Influence People by Dale Carnegie
Mr. Shmooze: The Art and Science of Selling Through Relationships by Richard Abraham
Raving Fans: A Revolutionary Approach to Customer Service by Ken Blanchard and Sheldon Bowles, with a foreword by Harvey Mackay
Switch: How to Change Things When Change Is Hard by Chip Heath and Dan Heath

FILMS

Pay It Forward is a 2000 American film about a seventh grade boy given a social studies assignment to launch a project that changes the world. The boy starts a "pay it forward" movement, which means paying back a debt not to the person whom you owe but to someone else, so it starts off a wave of selfless giving. The film inspires behavior based on responding to someone else's needs without focusing strictly on yourself.

Breaking Away is about four teenage boys in Bloomington, Indiana, who create their own relay team to compete in the famous Indiana University Little 500 bicycle race against professionals from around the world and, against all odds, win at the last second. The story is a beautifully acted portrayal of team work success, and ranked eighth on the list of America's 100 Most Inspiring Movies compiled by the American Film Institute.

Chariots of Fire is based on the true story of two runners from the University of Cambridge who compete together on the British team during the 1924 Olympics in Paris. One is a devout Scottish Christian who nearly ruins any chance for a medal by refusing to enter a race held on a Sunday. The other is a Jew who competes to silence prevailing anti-Semitism in England and Europe during this pre-WWII period. In the climactic finale, both win gold medals, inspiring the world with their altruism, self-sacrifice, and sense of universal brotherhood.

Working Girl is a film about cutthroat office politics inside the mergers and acquisitions department of a large Wall Street investment bank. A boss tries to take credit for her secretary's ideas, but ultimately is defeated by the spunk and intelligence of her younger rival. It demonstrates overcoming a tradition of a ruthless office culture by focusing solely on what's right for the customer.

The Blind Side is based on the true story of an impoverished black boy adopted by an affluent white Southern family and encouraged to play highly competitive football. As he gradually becomes successful we see how major community prejudice and widespread discrimination are confronted, with an inspiring and uplifting outcome.

First Position is a documentary film about preteen dancers from all over the world competing in the Youth America Grand Prix in New York City, an annual competition for dancers ages nine to nineteen for a place at an elite ballet school and company. It demonstrates the amazing, obsessive, and often painful self-discipline required of these children and their parents in the pursuit of artistic excellence and professional opportunity. The film's inspirational message can be applied to virtually all endeavor in building individual and team business success.

The Artist is a black-and-white French comedy-drama. The conflict of change is richly demonstrated as silent movies are replaced by "talkies." It reinforces the need for and the ultimate benefit of delivering what consumers want and having the willingness to accept needed changes.

RESOURCES

For speaking, consulting, and coaching inquiries, visit our websites: www.RichardWeylman.com or www.WeylmanConsultingGroup.com.

E-mail Richard at richard@richardweylman.com or call at 1-800-535-4332 and internationally at 941-828-3600.

To receive Richard's free bimonthly e-mailed business performance tips, enroll at www.RichardWeylman.com.

For additional book orders, visit https://richardweylman.com/the-power-of-why.

For other educational products, visit www.RichardWeylman.com.

For online learning, visit our online university website at www.WeylmanCenter.com.

Please send all other correspondence to our corporate headquarters at Weylman Consulting Group, c/o Richard Weylman, Inc., P.O. Box 510970, Punta Gorda, FL 33951.

Index

C. RICHARD WEYLMAN,
chairman of Weylman Consulting Group and
CEO of the Weylman Center for Excellence in
Practice Management, is a highly sought-after sales
and marketing consultant, speaker, and media ex-
pert. His writings have been featured in *Investment
Advisor, Fundfire, NALU, GAMA News Journal,*
and on WSJ.com and Forbes.com.

WeylmanConsultingGroup.com